A Well-Reasoned Opinion?
Critical Analysis of the First Case
Against the Alleged Senior Leaders
of the Khmer Rouge
(Case 002/01)

DAVID COHEN, MELANIE HYDE & PENELOPE VAN TUYL
with Stephanie Fung

EAST-WEST CENTER
COLLABORATION · EXPERTISE · LEADERSHIP

AIJI

WSD**HANDA**CENTER
FOR HUMAN RIGHTS & INTERNATIONAL JUSTICE
Stanford University

EAST-WEST CENTER
COLLABORATION · EXPERTISE · LEADERSHIP

The East-West Center promotes better relations and understanding among the people and nations of the United States, Asia, and the Pacific through cooperative study, research, and dialogue. Established by the US Congress in 1960, the Center serves as a resource for information and analysis on critical issues of common concern, bringing people together to exchange views, build expertise, and develop policy options.

The Center's 21-acre Honolulu campus, adjacent to the University of Hawai'i at Mānoa, is located midway between Asia and the US mainland and features research, residential, and international conference facilities. The Center's Washington, DC, office focuses on preparing the United States for an era of growing Asia Pacific prominence.

EastWestCenter.org

For information or to order copies, please contact:

Publications Office
East-West Center
1601 East-West Road
Honolulu, Hawai'i 96848-1601

Tel: 808.944.7145
Fax: 808.944.7376

EWCBooks@EastWestCenter.org
EastWestCenter.org/Publications

ISBN: 978-0-86638-270-0 (print) and 978-0-86638-271-7 (electronic)

© 2015 East-West Center

A Well-Reasoned Opinion? Critical Analysis of the First Case Against the Alleged Senior Leaders of the Khmer Rouge (Case 002/01) by David Cohen, Melanie Hyde & Penelope Van Tuyl with Stephanie Fung

Cover photographs: (top) Courtroom proceedings, the Extraordinary Chambers in the Courts of Cambodia (ECCC), by Nhet Sok Heng/ECCC; (bottom) 350 villagers from Takeo and 50 students from Phnom Penh visited the ECCC, photo courtesy of the ECCC.

Table of Contents

List of Figures and Tables

List of Acronyms

AIJI	Asian International Justice Initiative
CIJs	Co-Investigating Judges
CPK	Communist Party of Kampuchea
CPL	Civil Party Lawyer
CPLCL	Civil Party Lead Co-Lawyer
DC-Cam	Documentation Center of Cambodia
DK	Democratic Kampuchea
ECCC	Extraordinary Chambers in the Courts of Cambodia
ICC	International Criminal Court
ICTR	International Criminal Tribunal for Rwanda
ICTY	International Criminal Tribunal for the former Yugoslavia
IMT	International Military Tribunal at Nuremberg
IMTFE	International Military Tribunal for the Far East
IRs	Internal Rules
IS	Ieng Sary
ITU	Interpretation and Translation Unit
JCE	Joint Criminal Enterprise
KRT	Khmer Rouge Tribunal
KS	Khieu Samphan
NC	Nuon Chea
OCIJ	Office of the Co-Investigating Judges
OCP	Office of the Co-Prosecutors
PTC	Pre-Trial Chamber
RAK	Revolutionary Army of Kampuchea
SCC	Supreme Court Chamber
SCSL	Special Court for Sierra Leone
TC	Trial Chamber
TCCP	Trial Chamber Civil Party (witness)
TCE	Trial Chamber Expert (witness)
TCW	Trial Chamber Witness
UN	United Nations
US	United States
VSS	Victim Support Section
WWII	World War II

Executive Summary

On 7 August 2014, the Extraordinary Chambers in the Courts of Cambodia (ECCC) reached an important institutional milestone when the Court published its long-awaited Trial Judgment in the first case against two of the surviving alleged senior leaders of the Khmer Rouge—Nuon Chea and Khieu Samphan ("Case 002/01"). The Court found both men guilty of crimes against humanity, and sentenced them each to life imprisonment, while awarding "moral and collective reparations" to a consolidated group of Civil Parties participating in the trial. Despite hopes that the five-year process of judicial investigation, trial, deliberation, and Judgment-drafting would produce a rigorous and insightful final product, in reality, as this report argues, the Case 002/01 Judgment fails to deliver the most fundamental output one expects from a criminal trial—systematic application of the elements of crimes to a well-documented body of factual findings. Based, in part, on insight gained from the continuous presence of a team of trial monitors throughout the trial, this report provides commentary on how a contentious and confusing trial process in Case 002/01 ultimately produced a similarly troubled final Judgment.

Part I of the report provides context and a foundation for subsequent analysis, with a brief narrative overview of key developments during the trial. Part II focuses on critical analysis of trial procedure in Case 002/01, arguing that the Trial Chamber's poor handling of a number of novel and complex legal issues arising out of Case 002 created procedural confusion that permeated many aspects of the trial. This part of the report also traces important changes that the Tribunal implemented with respect to the victim participation scheme between Case 001 and Case 002, and assesses how the new framework impacted the trial, with a particular focus on trial efficiency, as well as the representation and meaningful participation of the Civil Parties during the trial. Finally, Part III undertakes a close reading of the Judgment itself, finding a great deal of cause for concern in the Court's analysis of the facts and application of the law, including the substantive legal analysis and factual findings underlying the Court's liability assessment.

Among the most important causes of the procedural confusion, which often overshadowed the substance of the trial proceedings, was the severance of what became Case 002/01 from the initially planned Case 002. This severance also had the effect of deferring the most important charges against the Accused to a future Case 002/02. While the massive scope of the Closing Order in Case 002 did present significant challenges in regard to trial management and the potential duration of the proceedings, the severance strategy adopted by the Trial Chamber was not successful in meeting those challenges. Indeed, severance of Case 002/01 had negative procedural and substantive repercussions, the effects of which are still being felt. The severance of Case 002/01 resulted in protracted uncertainty and created new trial management challenges that added significantly to the duration and complexity of the trial, rather than expediting it. The Parties challenged the validity of the Severance Order throughout the trial, and the Supreme Court Chamber eventually annulled the Order a year and a half into the proceedings. This ruling did not ultimately resolve any of the issues, however, because the Trial Chamber elected to subsequently re-sever the case in almost exactly the same way and continue the proceedings. The Supreme Court

Chamber had acknowledged the serious impact of leaving the scope of the charges unclear throughout the trial, but in the end nothing was done to address the consequences this had on Case 002/01. The decision of the Supreme Court Chamber to let the renewed severance stand indicates that pragmatism may have superseded concerns of justice and fairness in the proceedings.

Another cause of procedural controversy in the trial proceedings was the repeated concerns expressed at trial over the treatment of documentary evidence by the Trial Chamber, including the limitations the Chamber's procedural decisions placed on the right of confrontation in the name of expediency. For example, the Trial Chamber decided to admit a large body of prior statements into evidence without calling these witnesses to testify in Court, thus leaving this evidence largely untested. The Trial Chamber justified its decision, against Defense objections, with reference to expediency, and by saying that such testimony would not bear upon the alleged criminal conduct of the Accused as set out in the Closing Order. Our analysis of the Judgment, however, indicates that the Chamber did in fact rely repeatedly upon such statements to establish the administrative and communications structures of the Khmer Rouge. It then used these findings to infer the *de facto* control of the Accused over direct perpetrators of crimes, and this in turn formed the basis for convictions of the Accused under Joint Criminal Enterprise and Superior Responsibility theories. The Chamber reached these findings without any reference to corroborating evidence specific to the alleged criminal acts of the Accused. This manner of proceeding would thus appear to have denied the Accused meaningful rights of confrontation. It remains to be seen whether the Supreme Court Chamber will validate the Trial Chamber's prioritization of the right to an expeditious trial over other fair trial rights of the Accused.

The general response to all the Defense concerns on documentary evidence was a promise, repeated through the documentary hearing decisions and articulated again in the Judgment, that of course the Chamber would undertake a careful assessment of probative value of any evidence relied upon in the end. The Trial Chamber promised that it would consider all irregularities in witness interviews from the investigative phase, as well as discrepancies between these interviews and the testimony witnesses gave at trial, when determining the probative value and weight to be accorded to the evidence in the Judgment. However, the rest of the Judgment contains no actual explicit consideration of any Party objections to the probative value of evidence. There is a general recitation of the factors that are relevant to analyzing the probative value of evidence, but there are literally only a handful of instances in the rest of the 630-page Judgment where the Trial Chamber actually demonstrates this weighing of various factors in order to justify reliance on a particular piece of evidence. This is true for documentary and testimonial evidence from regular witnesses, expert witnesses, and Civil Parties alike. One is left to simply presume that the Chamber conducted such an analysis, although as will be discussed in Part III of this report, the quality of the factual findings and legal conclusions leave ample basis to doubt such analysis took place. To further complicate evidentiary matters, the Judgment also uses victim impact statements or statements of suffering to support its factual findings relevant to liability of the Accused, despite its previous assurances at trial that the sole purpose of the victim impact statements was to determine matters relevant to reparations and sentencing. The Chamber had assured the Defense that the statements would not be relevant to establishing the guilt of the Accused and, hence, on this basis denied the Defense an opportunity to confront consequential evidence.

In Part III of this report, we argue that the Case 002/01 Judgment is inadequate in its failure to meet expected standards for a final written reasoned decision. Sound legal judgments are based on a systematic application of the elements of crimes to a well-documented body of factual findings, reached through a careful analysis of the weight and credibility of the testimony and evidence bearing on each charge in the indictment, and taking into account the competing contentions of the Defense and Prosecution on each element. Falling far below this standard, the Judgment in Case 002/01 offers a poorly organized, ill-documented, and meandering narrative in lieu of clearly structured legal writing, based upon a thorough and balanced analysis of the legal and factual issues in dispute.

What distinguishes this Judgment from the standard practices of other tribunals is the lack of a coherent structure for organizing the evidence and analysis in a series of factual findings, based upon the elements in regard to each charge against the Accused. Also missing is a systematic weighing of that evidence based upon clearly articulated legal standards and a discussion of relative credibility. In the almost complete absence of such structured analysis, the basis of the factual findings scattered throughout the Judgment remains largely obscure. Narrative format operates to defeat the juristic analysis, which is the core of a well-reasoned opinion.

The Judgment repeatedly draws inferences from a factual narrative that assumes rather than justifies the validity of those inferences. This is particularly apparent in the treatment of the key issue as to what inferences can reasonably be drawn from the incomplete and often contradictory evidence about the attendance or participation of the Accused in key meetings of the Khmer Rouge leadership. Proof of guilt beyond a reasonable doubt requires a solid factual foundation of findings pointing to shared intent and effective control, which are essential elements of the theories of liability employed by the Judgment. Almost entirely lacking in the Chamber's treatment of this evidence is an analysis of whether those inferences and their factual basis meet the reasonable doubt standard of proof according to the systematic application of criteria for assessing credibility and probative value.

In addition to the lack of systematic and cogent analysis for the factual findings, the application of legal doctrines to the facts also provides cause for concern throughout the Judgment. In particular, the manner in which the Judgment employs Joint Criminal Enterprise and Superior Responsibility as key theories of liability reflects incomplete research, inaccuracies, and misapprehension of significant aspects of these doctrines and the applicable jurisprudence on which they are based. While this report asserts no conclusive opinion as to the ultimate question of the liability of the Accused, the serious shortcomings of the Judgment cannot be ignored. We offer the critical assessment herein with the hope that it will provide the basis for addressing these concerns in Case 002/02 and any subsequent trials at the ECCC.

A Well-Reasoned Opinion?
Critical Analysis of the First Case
Against the Alleged Senior Leaders
of the Khmer Rouge
(Case 002/01)

Part I: Introduction

On 7 August 2014, the Extraordinary Chambers in the Courts of Cambodia (ECCC) reached an important institutional milestone when the Court published its long-awaited Trial Judgment in the case against two of the surviving alleged senior leaders of the Khmer Rouge—Nuon Chea and Khieu Samphan.[1] The Court found both men guilty of crimes against humanity, and sentenced them each to life imprisonment,[2] while awarding "moral and collective reparations" to a consolidated group of Civil Parties[3] participating in the trial.[4] Defense teams for Khieu Samphan and Nuon Chea, as well as the ECCC Office of the Co-Prosecutors (OCP), have since filed appeals against numerous aspects of the Trial Judgment.[5] These are currently pending before the Tribunal's Supreme Court Chamber (SCC).

This was the second trial at the ECCC, and although more than five years had passed between the date the Judges were first sworn in[6] and the date substantive trial hearings began on 21 November 2011, the Tribunal, in many ways, remained an institution under development. Weeks into the Case 002 evidentiary hearings, the Chamber was still attempting to figure out the definitions and boundaries of its own trial procedure, while also fielding motions from the Parties over fundamental aspects of trial management.[7] The challenges apparent in ECCC operations are not unusual for specially constituted international tribunals—which operate under *sui generis* rules of procedure, and inevitably lack the clarity and specificity one can expect from a mature, permanent criminal justice system.[8] One might have expected that the ECCC would have made more progress in the first trial, working through many of the procedural questions that dogged Case 002, but Case 001 was a very different case from Case 002.

The Defendant in the first trial, Kaing Guek Eav, alias "Duch," actually admitted to the vast majority of the factual allegations against him. Although Duch asked to be acquitted of charges during his final week at trial, he largely cooperated with the Chamber throughout the proceedings. As a result, many of the procedures that became highly controversial during Case 002 were never seriously litigated in the Duch trial. Case 002 was also much larger and a far more complex case to litigate than Case 001 had been. The Duch trial began with an initial hearing on 17 February 2009, and concluded with closing statements later the same year, on 27 November. That trial spanned a total of 22 weeks (or 77 days), during which time the Chamber heard 9 expert witnesses, 17 fact witnesses, 7 character witnesses, and 22 Civil Parties.[9] Approximately 1,000 pieces of documentary evidence were put before the Chamber during the first trial.[10] In July 2010, Duch was convicted of crimes against humanity and grave breaches of the Geneva Conventions, and sentenced to a term of years in prison.[11] The Court awarded some limited "moral and collective reparations" to the Civil Parties, but rejected many of the specific reparations proposals for various reasons.[12]

By comparison, in January 2011 the ECCC Pre-Trial Chamber (PTC) confirmed a much more extensive Closing Order for Case 002. Whereas the Closing Order in the Duch case had been 45 pages long,[13] the Case 002 Closing Order ran nearly 800 pages long, indicting four new Accused—Ieng Sary, Ieng Thirith, Khieu Samphan, and Nuon Chea—for crimes against humanity and grave breaches of the Geneva Conventions, as well as for genocide.[14] The scope of factual inquiry reflected in the Case 002 Closing Order also reached much farther than Case 001 had done. Whereas the Duch case was primarily about events in, around, and related to one major Khmer Rouge detention center, known as "S-21," the subject matter of the charges in Case 002 spanned the entire country, throughout the entire period of Democratic Kampuchea (DK) (17 April 1975 to 6 January 1979).

In addition to the more voluminous Case File and farther-reaching charges in Case 002, the role of victim participants shifted dramatically between Case 001 and Case 002. The Internal Rules (IRs) adopted by the ECCC largely mirror the civil law system that Cambodia inherited from the French during colonial rule. In accordance with this system, victims with civil claims against an accused person may be parties to the criminal proceeding, enjoying many of the same rights as the Defense and Prosecution.[15] This "Civil Party" system was heralded by many as a milestone in victim's rights—going, in many respects, above and beyond the victim participation scheme implemented at the permanent International Criminal Court.[16] However, during Case 001, the practical difficulties in applying this sort of participatory scheme to mass crimes soon became apparent. Moreover, the number of Civil Party applications pending in Case 002 was around 60 times the size of the already very time-consuming pool in Case 001 (76 Civil Parties were admitted in Case 001, compared with 3,869 ultimately admitted in Case 002).

Partly in an attempt to manage these practical challenges, no fewer than eight revisions were made to the Internal Rules between 2007 and 2011.[17] Following the substantial amendments introduced in the fifth revision of the Internal Rules, the victim participation scheme appeared to move away from the original notion of Civil Parties as "fully fledged" parties to the proceedings.[18] This transformation offered less individualized representation of Civil Parties and more symbolic representation of the collective group. Meanwhile, the Court's shifting approach to Civil Party engagement also left many open questions throughout the second trial about procedural rules for confronting and examining Civil Party testimony, as well as fair trial concerns arising out of how the Court would use evidence provided by Civil Parties in the final assessment of factual and legal findings in the Judgment.[19]

Trial proceedings in Case 002 commenced in April 2011, when a trial management meeting was called to confront how best to organize the proceedings, since the Parties had requested to hear testimony from

1,054 witnesses and tender approximately 7,600 proposed documents into evidence. Several of the Accused had also challenged their own mental and physical fitness to stand trial in pre-trial motions, so the Court appointed medical experts to assess these Accused.[20] During initial hearings in late June 2011, the Chamber directed the Parties to indicate "priority witnesses, experts, and Civil Parties" prior to the beginning of the trial to be called to give testimony. Parties also made submissions of preliminary objections to jurisdiction.[21] Within the next three months, the Trial Chamber issued decisions on those objections it considered a barrier to the commencement of evidentiary hearings.[22] All other matters were deferred to the end of trial.

Concerned about the size and scope of the case, the age and ill health of the Accused, and the prospects for completing a trial through to Judgment,[23] the Trial Chamber abruptly announced a controversial plan in September 2011 to separate ("sever") the charges in the Case 002 Closing Order into a series of smaller trials, divided by subject matter. Having never invited the Parties to make any submissions on the matter, the Trial Chamber issued a four-page Severance Order, pursuant to Internal Rule 89*ter*, limiting the scope of inquiry in the first trial (now known as "Case 002/01") to the following subject matter: [24]

- The structure of Democratic Kampuchea;
- Roles of each Accused during the period prior to the establishment of Democratic Kampuchea, including when these roles were assigned;
- Role of each Accused in the Democratic Kampuchean government, their assigned responsibilities, the extent of their authority and the lines of communication throughout the temporal period with which the ECCC is concerned;
- Policies of Democratic Kampuchea;
- Factual allegations described in the Closing Order as movement of population (phases one and two)[25] and crimes against humanity committed in their course, including murder, extermination, persecution (except on religious grounds), forced transfer, and enforced disappearances.

Over a year later (8 October 2012), the Trial Chamber would also add the executions of former Khmer Republic officials at Tuol Po Chrey to the scope of the Severance Order, in partial response to a Prosecution motion asking for a much broader, more representative sampling of the crime scenes that had been included in the full Closing Order for Case 002.[26] Other charges related to worksites, cooperatives, forced marriage, security centers and execution sites, as well as forced movements from the Eastern Zone (referred to in the Closing Order as "Phase Three") were left out of the first severed trial, as were all allegations of genocide and persecution on religious grounds as a crime against humanity. Grave breaches of the Geneva Conventions were also deferred to an unspecified future trial, which most commentators and many within the Tribunal seemed dubious would ever take place.[27]

Severance was ostensibly meant to create efficiency, but given the way it was executed, it actually occasioned a great deal of procedural uncertainty and triggered many new trial management challenges, which arguably created more inefficiency in the end. Severing a complex trial in this particular way was completely without precedent in international criminal trial practice. The severance was also criticized by the Parties and by outside observers for being unrepresentative. Nonetheless, at the time of severance, the Trial Chamber denied all objections and requests for reconsideration of scope.[28] On 17 November 2011, Ieng Thirith was deemed unfit to stand trial due to dementia (likely Alzheimer's). The charges against her were further severed from Case 002, and a stay of proceedings against her was granted.[29] At the same time, Nuon Chea was deemed fit to stand trial, so with three remaining co-defendants, Case 002/01 commenced with Opening Statements on 21 November 2011.

Even as hearings began, the Parties continued to object to the lack of clarity in the Severance Order. Persistent debates arose in Court around the scope of permissible questioning, legal submissions, and documentary evidence in light of the severance.[30] Incredibly, the validity of this Order, and by extension the scope of the charges, remained a contested legal matter through the *entire* duration of the trial.[31] The Prosecution persisted with motions for reconsideration of scope,[32] ultimately appealing the issue to the SCC. This appeal formed the basis for an SCC decision vacating the Severance Order nearly a year and a half into the trial.[33] Following this decision by the SCC, the Trial Chamber was compelled quite belatedly to invite submissions from the Parties on the proper scope of the trial that was already well underway. On 29 March 2013, the Chamber re-severed Case 002 with a virtually identical scope articulated for Case 002/01, but with a much more clearly articulated and representatively sampled scope of charges outlined for a subsequent Case 002/02.[34] The OCP and the Nuon Chea Defense immediately appealed the renewed Severance Order, but this time the SCC dismissed the appeals and allowed the severance to stand. The SCC handed its decision down on 23 July 2013—the same day evidentiary hearings concluded in Case 002/01.[35]

The struggles with severance and defining a manageable scope for the trial illustrate a major issue international criminal tribunals have dealt with for decades: how to manage major mass atrocity cases, which are unwieldy to try given the large number of victims and crime sites, the temporal and geographic span of events, as well as the sheer volume of evidence. The ECCC faced additional layers of difficulty with the lapse of three decades since the crimes were committed, creating problems arising from old evidence, old witnesses, and old defendants. Added complexity arose from the truly hybrid legal nature of the Tribunal, mixing Cambodian domestic procedure from the continental European civil law tradition with practice in other international tribunals, which have tended to follow Anglo-American adversarial procedural models. These practical challenges should not have taken Court officials by surprise, and yet the ECCC often appeared to be operating reactively to fundamental trial management questions, which made for a procedurally confusing trial experience for the Parties and outside observers alike.

Frustration over the lack of clear parameters for the trial and confusion over trial procedure boiled over repeatedly in Court. Over the course of the trial there were formal complaints lodged for professional misconduct against various Defense Counsel for flouting decorum in the Trial Chamber.[36] There were also motions filed to remove sitting Judges for bias. There were many weeks where trial monitors reported on a breakdown of courtroom decorum in the midst of tense and exasperated exchanges between Parties and the Chamber.[37] Such exchanges sometimes led to further controversy, such as when the Trial Chamber began switching off the microphone of various Defense Counsel when they tried to continue making arguments the Trial Chamber no longer wished to hear.[38] Confusion and frustration were also readily apparent in the written filings attendant to the proceedings, with controversy arising over an unusual Trial Chamber practice of responding to multiple Party motions at once with short "Memos" rather than the more typical reasoned Decision or Order.[39]

The financial circumstances of the Tribunal throughout Case 002/01 must be acknowledged as well, as they certainly cannot have helped the Court navigate the voluminous evidentiary record or respond efficiently to the many pressing procedural motions. As an institution funded by voluntary contributions, the Court found itself unable to pay its own staff—particularly those hired on the national side of the

Tribunal—a number of times during the course of Case 002/01. Article 44 in Law on the Establishment of ECCC stipulates that the expenses and salaries of the Cambodian staff, including national judges and prosecutors, shall be borne by the Cambodian national budget, while the international staff salaries shall be borne by the United Nations (UN).[40] However, in practice, salaries on both the national and international sides have been largely funded by voluntary contributions from donor governments throughout the ECCC's existence. Accordingly, for much of Case 002, the Court has operated under what has aptly been described as a "chronic and increasingly disruptive financial crisis."[41]

Problems with lack of necessary technical, legal, and administrative ECCC staff certainly impacted the speed of the trial. In October 2012, the Chamber reduced the number of days the Court sat to just three days a week.[42] After the death of Ieng Sary in March 2013 and a hearing on Nuon Chea's fitness to stand trial, the proceedings noticeably picked up pace, with the Trial Chamber returning to sitting four days a week most weeks through July 2013. However, twice during this period, acute funding difficulties seriously disrupted the Court's operations. A nearly $3 million shortfall in budget contributions from the Cambodian government in 2013 led to many months without pay for the national staff of the ECCC, from December 2012 through February 2013. In protest, members of the absolutely vital Interpretation and Translation Unit (ITU) staged an unprecedented "work boycott" at the beginning of March, right in the middle of Case 002/01 proceedings.[43] The situation was temporarily resolved by additional contributions secured from international donors,[44] but later the same year national staff again went unpaid for several months. This led to a larger-scale national staff strike after the close of evidentiary hearings, and during the deliberations. In that strike, 134 national staff members did not report for duty.[45] The second crisis was temporarily resolved through a combination of exceptionally granted bridge funds from the UN and foreign national governments to pay the salaries in arrears, alongside a $1.8 million pledge from the Cambodian government to cover national salaries through the end of 2013.[46] However, as the Deputy Secretary General of the United Nations, Jan Eliasson, said in an address to the Fall 2013 Pledging Conference for the ECCC:

> The impact on the work of the ECCC of such stoppages, both in the past and anticipated, is self-evident. No justice institution, let alone one adjudicating international crimes of the utmost gravity, should have to cope with such uncertainties. The detrimental effect of financially induced stoppages is particularly critical in light of ongoing judicial proceedings.[47]

Case 002/01 ended with closing statements on 31 October 2013. In total, the ECCC Trial Chamber had presided over 222 trial days within a two-year period. During that time, the case lost another Accused, Ieng Sary, who died midway through trial, in March 2013. A total of 92 individuals testified during Case 002/01, including 3 experts, 53 fact witnesses, 5 character witnesses, and 31 Civil Parties (of the 3,869 admitted to the proceedings).[48] In place of oral testimony, and over the strong objections of Defense Counsel, the Chamber also admitted 1,124 written records of interviews with witnesses and Civil Parties who were not called to Court to be examined during the trial.[49] These were part of a collection of more than 5,800 documents that were admitted into evidence, reportedly amounting to more than 222,000 pages counting all translations into the three official languages of the Court (Khmer, English, and French).[50] Also in this body of documentary evidence were 46 written records of interviews with the Charged Persons, reports on crime sites, demographic data, and medical evidence.[51]

Ten months after the closing arguments, the Trial Chamber published its 630 page Judgment in Case 002/01. On 7 August 2014, world media packed into the ECCC pressroom to report on the historic verdict in this case. From this news coverage, casual observers would have heard that Khieu Samphan and Nuon Chea were convicted of multiple crimes against humanity, primarily pursuant to a Joint Criminal Enterprise (JCE) theory of liability, and sentenced to serve life in prison. They would also likely have heard about how the Court awarded "moral and collective reparations" to nearly 4,000 victims participating in the trial as Civil Parties. What they would not have heard is any real critical analysis of the quality of the Judgment itself, much less any in-depth reflection on the trial that produced it.

This report is not meant to be a comprehensive retrospective on the entire trial, detailing every noteworthy development or controversy.[52] Rather, the report takes as a starting point the long-awaited, highly anticipated Judgment in Case 002/01, which an objective reader would have to acknowledge was poorly written and well below the standard of most of the other international criminal tribunals. One might have hoped that a five-year process of judicial investigation, trial, deliberation, and Judgment-drafting would produce a more rigorous final product. Unfortunately, as a piece of legal writing, the Case 002/01 Judgment is inadequate in its failure to meet expected standards for a final written reasoned decision. Sound legal judgments are based on a systematic application of the elements of crimes to a well-documented body of factual findings, reached through a careful analysis of the weight and credibility of the testimony and other evidence bearing on each charge in the indictment, and taking into account the competing contentions of Defense and Prosecution on each element. Falling far below this standard, the Judgment in Case 002/01 offers a poorly organized, meandering narrative in lieu of clearly structured legal writing, based upon a thorough and balanced analysis of the legal and factual issues in dispute.

Documents such as the Case 002/01 Judgment can only be understood in the context of the concrete institution and trial proceedings that produced them. A criminal trial is meant to follow a highly structured process of inquiry, constrained by a principled set of rules. The procedural constraints exist to keep the trial fair, while ensuring a systematic inquiry into all available facts, a transparent application of the relevant law, and legal and factual findings based upon a reasoned and objective analysis of the available evidence. Strong faith in the fairness of the proceedings allows participants and observers of a trial to trust the merit of the conclusions published in the final Judgment. Of course, the inverse is also true, so it should come as no surprise that the contentious and confusing trial process in Case 002/01 would produce a similarly troubled final Judgment.

Part II: Critical Analysis of Trial Procedure

The trial was marked by procedural confusion in a number of realms, stemming at least in part from the Trial Chamber's questionable handling of several novel and complex legal issues arising out of Case 002. Three particularly salient issues, touched upon briefly in the introduction, merit more detailed discussion because they provide important context for the nature of the fact-finding process the Trial Chamber undertook during the trial, which formed the basis for the final Judgment. Moreover, they offer insight into the environment in which contentious legal issues were litigated before the Chamber. In this section, we consider: (1) persistent confusion throughout the trial about the impact of the severance on the substantive scope of the trial and the fair trial rights of the Accused; (2) the implications of the Trial Chamber's approach to management of a voluminous body of documentary evidence; and (3) the impact of a new and unfamiliar framework for Civil Party engagement following a major structural reorganization between Case 001 and Case 002.

SEVERANCE

The severance of Case 002 had serious implications for trial management. There were obvious practical challenges to the implementation of the Severance Order when it came to limiting the scope of witness examination or determining the admissibility of documentary evidence. This was compounded by the fact that the Parties challenged the validity of the Severance Order throughout the trial. The Order was in fact annulled by the Supreme Court Chamber a year and a half after the trial began, although the Trial Chamber was then allowed to re-sever the case in exactly the same way, over the objections of the Parties. This meant there was protracted uncertainty about the scope of the charges, lasting from the beginning of trial all the way to the final day.

Practical Challenges to Implementation

Trial monitors observed countless interruptions to courtroom proceedings that were linked to confusion over the practical implications of the severance. From the first day of evidentiary hearings, the parameters for the questioning of Civil Parties and witnesses were manifestly unclear. In fact, almost every individual called to testify (whether categorized as a Civil Party or an ordinary witness) triggered questions and objections from the Parties about whether the testimony was out of scope. Part of the confusion arose because the Trial Chamber had ruled early in the trial that some testimony, in exceptional circumstances, would be allowed to go beyond the scope outlined in the Severance Order.[53] The Parties frequently raised objections and sought clarification about what constituted "exceptional circumstances" under which the Trial Chamber allowed the Parties to ask questions beyond the strict scope of the first trial.

Parties were also uncertain about whether or not they could discuss other topics beyond the strict scope of severance, if they did so for the purpose of providing context to the crimes alleged, the administrative and communications structures, or the policies of the Communist Party of Kampuchea (CPK), all of which did fall within the scope of Case 002/01.[54] Lack of clarity in the original Severance Order was compounded by inconsistent rulings by the Court throughout proceedings as they determined on a case-by-case basis what was allowable and what was not. Accordingly, Defense Counsel, Civil Party representatives, and OCP lawyers argued continuously in Court over whether certain topics—such as dam worksites, S-21, purges, events before 1975 and after 1976, religious persecution, and forced marriage—fell outside of the scope of the first trial, or were linked sufficiently to the topics that fell within the scope of the trial.

Exchanges of this type continued even up to the final days of the two-year trial, as the Parties sought clarification and decisive rulings. A few specific examples illustrate the deep confusion and frustration the severance created. During week 41 of evidentiary hearings, the President had to repeatedly remind the Prosecution to limit its examination to questions related to the first and second phases of evacuation. Prosecutor Raynor argued that the OCP's questions were relevant because they involved the authority and communication structures in the DK regime, which he called an "overarching principle" of Case 002/01. In response to this, Andrew Ianuzzi, Defense Counsel to Nuon Chea at the time, declared that Raynor's submissions depended on whether the Court accepted the "fiction" that there would be further Case 002 mini-trials.[55]

In week 52 of trial, the President of the Chamber maintained a close check on subjects straying outside of the case's scope—such as the evacuation of Kampot, the war with Vietnam in 1978, and forced marriage—while the Court granted more leeway with questions on purges. The Defense objected several times to OCP questioning on purging, but the Court did not sustain these objections on the grounds that, although the questions were related to purging, they were relevant to the implementation of CPK policy.[56] Similarly, during the last document hearing for Case 002/01, Defense Counsel for Khieu Samphan, Anta Guissé, raised several objections to the admissibility of documents pertaining to implementation of policy versus the existence of policy. This came up at least twice that week with documents presented by the OCP. While the OCP attempted to define the two ideas as separate things, Anta Guissé maintained that implementation and existence are conceptually inseparable in evidence put before the Court. Both she and Defense Counsel Victor Koppe displayed intense frustration with the Court's application of the Severance Order in that week.[57]

Protracted Uncertainty about the Scope of Charges

Further compounding the confusion about the practical consequences of the severance was the fact that Party challenges to the scope of charges included within the Severance Order remained a contested legal issue throughout the *entire* duration of Case 002/01. The principal criticism, espoused by all the Parties, was that the severance decision was unrepresentative of the charges in the Case File.[58] On 3 October 2011, the OCP filed a "Request for Reconsideration" of the Severance Order asking for the inclusion of a more representative selection of charges, raising concerns that Case 002/01 would be "the first and likely only trial" that the elderly Accused would face.[59] Arguing that "the first trial would not safeguard the fundamental interest of victims to achieve meaningful and timely justice nor would the Severance Order, as proposed, safeguard the right of all Accused in Case 002 to an expeditious trial," the filing proposed an alternative form of severance which would be more representative of the allegations but could be heard in a "similar time frame as that envisaged in the Severance Order."[60] However, on 18 October 2011, the Trial Chamber rejected this alternative severance proposal, which had included the addition of numerous crime sites.[61]

The trial continued, but the Prosecution submitted another proposal on 27 January 2012 asking again for an expansion of crime sites, including:

- The District 12 execution site ("District 12")
- The Tuol Po Chrey execution site ("Tuol Po Chrey," where hundreds of Khmer Republic soldiers and officials were allegedly executed by Khmer Rouge forces); and
- The S-21 security center (also known as Tuol Sleng), including the purges of cadres from the New North, Central (Old North) and East Zones sent to S-21, but excluding the Prey Sar worksite.[62]

Both Nuon Chea and Ieng Sary's Defense teams also urged the Trial Chamber to reconsider the Severance Order, arguing that Case 002 should be heard in its entirety.[63] However, the Nuon Chea Defense also argued that the issues of S-21 and internal purges are not relevant to the crimes of Case 002/01.[64] Khieu Samphan contended that trial issues should not be severed, but sought for his case to be severed from that of his co-Accused.[65] These motions remained pending for over seven months, while the trial continued. On 8 October 2012, the Trial Chamber released its second severance decision, in which they granted a modest expansion of the scope of the trial to include the killings of Khmer Republic soldiers at Tuol Po Chrey insofar as they occurred immediately after the evacuation of Phnom Penh.[66] The Trial Chamber decided this time limit would exclude killings that occurred between 1976 and 1977.[67]

Still dissatisfied, the OCP appealed to the SCC.[68] Three months after that appeal, the SCC issued a decision annulling the Severance Order nearly a year and a half into the trial.[69] The 8 February 2013 SCC Decision identified a number of errors of law in how the Trial Chamber undertook the severance process. The SCC criticized the failure to consult with the Parties on the terms and scope of the severance, as well as the lack of reasoning offered by the Order regarding "how the severance advances the interests of the justice."[70] The SCC determined that by neglecting to seek prior adversarial submissions about a possible severance, the Trial Chamber had violated the Parties' right to a reasoned opinion and their right to be heard, and that this decision, along with numerous subsequent errors in the exercise of the Trial Chamber's discretion, caused prejudice.[71]

The SCC explicitly acknowledged that the ongoing uncertainty about the scope of the case *as the case was being tried* was clearly a problem:

> It is also noteworthy that the Trial Chamber's invitation for submissions on the scope of Case 002/01, and the resultant Impugned Decision denying expansion in large part, came approximately one year after the issuance of the Severance Order. In the meantime, the Trial Chamber kept the limits of the scope of Case 002/01 in a state of uncertainty, and no plan was ever put into place regarding the number or scope of the remaining cases to be tried in Case 002. The latter situation remains true today, despite the Trial Chamber's indication in the Severance Order that "further information regarding subsequent cases to be tried in the course of Case 002 will be provided to the parties and the public in due course." [72]

The Supreme Court Chamber further determined that, despite an indication in the first Severance Order that, "further information regarding subsequent cases to be tried in the course of Case 002 will be provided to the parties and the public in due course," the Trial Chamber had not provided any clear or specific information as to the number, scope, or duration of trials envisaged after the first trial, and that such failure to create a plan regarding the handling of the remaining charges to be tried in Case 002 had also caused prejudice. The Supreme Court Chamber decided that the cumulative effect of the errors committed by the Trial Chamber occasioned the invalidity of the first severance of Case 002.

The SCC ruled that the Trial Chamber must reassess its approach to the Severance after inviting submissions from the Parties, balancing "all parties' respective interests" against "all relevant factors," and articulating a concrete future plan for adjudicating any charges excluded from the first trial.[73]

The Trial Chamber responded to the SCC decision immediately. The Chamber "scheduled a hearing and provided a list of nine detailed and specific issues related to the potential re-severance of Case 002 for the Parties to address, which they did on 18 and 20 February 2013. Following the submissions heard on 18 February 2013, the Trial Chamber issued another memorandum on 19 February 2013 requesting supplementary information related to the possible scope of a potential first trial, which the parties provided during a further hearing on 21 February 2013."[74] After this flurry of consultation, which had been mandated by the SCC, the Trial Chamber continued hearing evidence in Case 002/01, as it was formulating its decision on how to proceed with respect to severance. In light of the obvious uncertainty the SCC annulment cast on the proceedings, the Defense teams all argued that no witnesses, including Expert Witnesses Philip Short and Elizabeth Becker, should be called until the Trial Chamber had responded with a full and reasoned decision on the scope of the trial.[75]

On 29 March 2013, the Trial Chamber announced orally that it had decided to re-sever Case 002. Dismissing the notion of "representativeness of the Indictment" as meaningless, the Chamber indicated that the renewed severance would contain a scope of charges for Case 002/01 that was effectively identical to the 8 October 2012 version of severance.[76] The Chamber would still consider only charges related to Phase One and Phase Two movements, as well as a temporally limited scope of crimes alleged at Tuol Po Chrey. The Judges declared their intention to resume the proceedings from the point it had reached to that date. During the week of 8 to 12 April 2013, Counsel for Khieu Samphan, Arthur Vercken, objected to the continuation of proceedings in the absence of the Chamber's written reasoned decision on the renewal of severance. In that week, Prosecutor de Wilde d'Estmael also asked for some direction from the Chamber as to whether the Parties were to proceed on the basis of the paragraphs of the Closing Order listed in the annulled decision as relevant for Case 002/01. The President gave no indication when the written decision would be issued, but confirmed that the Case 002/01-relevant paragraphs of the Closing Order would be identical to those listed in the Severance Order annulled by the SCC.[77] The Trial Chamber provided its written reasons for this decision at the end of the month, on 26 April 2013.[78]

The OCP and the Nuon Chea Defense immediately appealed. The appeals argued that the Trial Chamber had failed to ensure the representativeness of the charges in Case 002/01.[79] They urged the SCC to expand the scope of the trial. The OCP sought to include charges related to S-21. The Nuon Chea Defense requested the annulment of the decision with prejudice to future severance orders, and argued in the alternative that, if the decision were not annulled, "reasonable representativeness" required the inclusion of genocide charges, as well as some crimes alleged at cooperatives and work sites.[80]

Although the renewed severance of the case by the Trial Chamber was effectively identical, the SCC did not annul the decision on second appeal. On 23 July 2013, the SCC issued a summary of reasons for dismissing the immediate appeals by the OCP and the Nuon Chea Defense against the Trial Chamber's second decision on severance.[81] The Chamber acknowledged that it "considers that the Trial Chamber's failure to comply with its instructions constitute an error of law and an error in the exercise of its discretion."[82] Nonetheless, the SCC declared that the Severance Order "was not so unreasonable as to warrant appellate intervention."[83] Ultimately, it seems clear from the text of the decision that the SCC took a pragmatic approach in response to the apparent fact that the Trial Chamber was not in fact prepared to adjudicate any of the broader charges in the Closing Order:

> Considering the advanced age of the accused and their deteriorating health, the notion of representativeness of the Indictment is valid for the question of severance of Case 002 in so far as it determines priority in addressing the severed charges. Case 002/01 could be reasonably representative of the Indictment not just by expanding its scope to include S-21, as per the Co-Prosecutors' request, but also by including the genocide charges, a cooperative, and a worksite, as per NUON Chea's request. However, the fact that, despite having spent 14 months preparing for the trial in Case 002, and having kept the scope of Case 002/01 open to change for a year, the Trial Chamber still declines to adjust its original position on severance in order to accommodate the parties' requests and address any of the parties concerns with the consequences of renewed severance for any future trials, suggests that the Trial Chamber may be unprepared to adjudicate the remaining charges in the Closing Order within Case 002/01.[84]

The solution the SCC settled for in light of the glaring inadequacies of the Trial Chamber's renewed Severance Order is articulated succinctly at Paragraph 11 of this decision:

> In the present circumstances, concerns of the effective management of the entirety of charges pending before the Trial Chamber prevail over the postulate that Case 002/01 be reasonably representative of the Indictment. The Supreme Court Chamber therefore considers that a more appropriate course of action at this stage is to instruct that charges that should have been included within the scope of Case 002/01 will instead form part of the scope of Case 002/02, so as to render the combination of Cases 002/01 and 002/02 reasonably representative of the Indictment. [85]

Thus, in its denial of appeal, the SCC revealed that perhaps what it had been most concerned about was that there be a concrete plan for trying the remaining issues in the Closing Order. Accordingly, the Decision declared that charges in Case 002/02 must at least include charges related to S-21, a worksite, a cooperative, and genocide.[86]

Impact of the Severance on Efficiency

Severance was ostensibly meant to create efficiency, but as seen in the discussion above, given the way it was executed, it actually occasioned a great deal of procedural uncertainty and triggered many new trial management challenges, which arguably created more inefficiency in the end. Beyond the inefficiencies it created within Case 002/01, one must also consider the broader implications of trying to orchestrate sequential trials from a single indictment. At the time of severance, nobody knew what the legal significance would be of holdings from the first Judgment in any hypothetical subsequent phases of trial. Would they be subject to *res judicata*? Would witnesses with testimony relevant to both stages of trial have to return twice to testify about the acts and conduct of the Accused and their role in the Khmer Rouge? What about the potential issue of prejudice of the Judges if they convicted the Accused in the first trial and then presided over a subsequent trial with the same Accused? These questions remained unanswered for a protracted period of time.

As the Nuon Chea Defense argued in its appeal against the second severance, neither the original Severance Order of the Trial Chamber, nor the renewed severance post-SCC appeal articulated "a plan sufficient to resolve the legal and practical impediments to holding sequential trials at the ECCC."[87] Perhaps the lack of planning was a product of the apparent belief at the time of severance that there might not ever be a second trial in sequence. However, by the end of Case 002/01, the two remaining defendants were still alive, and the financial crises the Court had faced in the second year of the trial appeared to have abated (at least temporarily). The SCC ordered that Case 002/02 was to commence as soon as possible after the closing submissions in Case 002/01. Recognizing that overlapping sequential trials put an unforeseen administrative burden on the Court, the SCC suggested empaneling additional Trial Judges in order expedite the trial process:

> Case 002/02 must therefore commence as soon as possible. The Supreme Court Chamber considers that the establishment of a second panel in order to achieve this has now become imperative. The Supreme Court Chamber accordingly instructs the Office of Administration of the ECCC to immediately explore the establishment of a second panel of national and international judges within the Trial Chamber to hear and adjudicate Case 002/02.[88]

Ultimately, no separate chamber of judges was ever empaneled for Case 002/02, but it bears noting that the SCC surprisingly made no consideration of the corresponding burden the Parties would face juggling overlapping trials.[89] As it happened, the appellate stage of Case 002/01 did overlap with the opening stage of Case 002/02. The Defense objected that it was impossible to simultaneously pursue the two proceedings in tandem, and actually successfully boycotted the 002/02 proceedings until the appeal was filed at the end of December 2014.[90] Considering that efficiency was one of the arguments in favor of severing the cases into smaller sub-parts, the interruptions to questioning throughout the trial, the temporary suspension of trial in Case 002/01 following the SCC's severance annulment, and the subsequent Defense boycott and attendant delay in Case 002/02 all illustrate the ways in which it may have had the opposite effect.

Apart from these delays, the SCC decision may even have created redundancies between Case 002/01 and Case 002/02. Despite the uncertainty about whether the general issues litigated in Case 002/01 would be applied to Case 002/02 as *res judicata*, the ECCC in fact declared that each trial would need to be treated separately, and each issue open to re-litigation. Thus, as recently as October 2014, the Trial Chamber was seised of motions from the Parties requesting further clarification on the extent to which Case 002/01 would serve as a foundation for Case 002/02.[91] In a Memo response, the Trial Chamber distilled the following guiding points from five separate sources, including oral decisions and prior written decisions of the Trial Chamber, as well as a July 2014 SCC decision on the matter:

> For the benefit of the Parties, the Chamber nevertheless wishes to distill the following key points from the SCC decision and remind the Parties of related relevant guidance provided by this Chamber:
>
> - The Case File remains the same for each trial in Case 002.
> - The evidence admitted in Case 002/01 is common to Case 002/02, with the effect

that evidence already put before the Chamber or heard in Case 002/01 will be maintained in Case 002/02. This includes both testimonial and documentary evidence.

- There is therefore no formal need to renew any assessment of admissibility concerning such evidence. The E3 numbers assigned to evidence during the proceedings in Case 002/01 will remain the same in Case 002/02. Similarly, the testimonies heard during Case 002/01 will remain part of the evidence available in Case 002/02.

- However, and in order to ensure a full adversarial debate, questions of relevance may be raised and the parties will be afforded the opportunity to test and challenge evidence already put before the Chamber in Case 002/01 insofar as it relates to the new charges in Case 002/02.

- Findings made in Case 002/01 including those based on evidence also relevant to Case 002/02 do not bind the Chamber, and common factual elements in all cases resulting from Case 002 will be established anew.

- The Chamber will not import any attribution of criminal responsibility from Case 002/01 into Case 002/02.[92]

DOCUMENTARY EVIDENCE

Another area of trial procedure that merits close scrutiny is the way in which the Court managed a voluminous body of documentary evidence, and the extent to which it struggled to balance the sometimes competing imperatives of efficiency and fairness. At the ECCC, documents admitted into evidence during the trial stage can come from the "Case File," or they can be put before the Chamber *propio motu* or by one of the Parties, during the course of the trial.[93] The Case File is a voluminous collection of evidentiary materials compiled by the Office of the Co-Investigating Judges (OCIJ) during the investigative stage of the proceedings. Based on what should be an exhaustive review of the evidence on the Case File, the Co-Investigative Judges will either conclude the investigation with a dismissal of charges or a Closing Order to indict, and then move to trial. For a piece of documentary evidence to form the basis of a factual finding in the Judgment, it must have been "put before the Chamber" during the trial proceedings, pursuant to IR 87(3). In other words, not all the materials from the Case File will be relied upon by the Chamber to determine the guilt or innocence of the Accused.

The exact modalities for putting documents before the Trial Chamber were a recurring concern in Case 001. The process under Rule 87(3) in the third revision of the Internal Rules[94] had proved to be both "tedious and time consuming."[95] Thus, on 11 June 2009, after almost three months of trial in Case 001, the ECCC held a Trial Management Meeting to address the inefficiency of the procedure. This resulted in the amendment of, among others, Rule 87(3). The amended language added "appropriately identified in court" as a way in which evidence from the Case File could be considered properly "put before the Chamber" for the purposes of IR 87(3). While the amendment facilitated a more efficient process of putting documents before the Chamber, the practical application of Rule 87(3) and the meaning of "appropriately identified in court" continued to be the subject of debate and confusion.

Building the Case File at the Investigative Stage

Because the investigative stages of criminal proceedings are confidential in the civil law system (after which the ECCC is most closely modeled), the Case File is also confidential. A "charged person" (who becomes known as an "Accused" only if subsequently indicted in the Closing Order) gains access to the Case File when charged at the beginning of the investigative stage, and may access it throughout the investigation. In Case 002, Nuon Chea gained access to the Case File on 19 September 2007 and Khieu Samphan gained access on 19 November 2007.[96] However, notwithstanding this access to documents placed on the Case File, at the ECCC the Defense is afforded no right to conduct its own investigations, and is excluded from the investigative interviews of the Co-Investigating Judges (CIJs). The Defense may file requests for investigative action by the OCIJ, but if the OCIJ refuses to pursue a line of investigation, the Defense cannot act independently—as it could in a typical adversarial system—to prepare for trial by marshaling evidence to support the Defense arguments or impeach credibility. The Nuon Chea Defense complained throughout the trial that the exclusion of Defense Counsel from investigative interviews was the first step in a series of procedural decisions with respect to documentary evidence that operated to impede the ability of the Accused to mount an effective defense:

> The investigation was conducted in conditions of absolute secrecy. Contrary to standard practice in civil law systems, Defence counsel was excluded from the CIJs' interviews completely. Defence teams were also prohibited from, and indeed sanctioned for, conducting their own investigations. For more than two years of the three-year investigation, the CIJs refused to provide basic information about the general direction and strategy of the investigation or the standard operating procedures of its investigators.[97]

Early in the investigative stage, in January of 2008, OCIJ sent a memorandum to all Defense teams explaining the decision to exclude them from witness interviews, by asserting that there is no absolute right of confrontation at the investigative stage of the proceedings. However, the OCIJ assured the Defense that "for that reason, Rule [84(1)] recognizes the right of the accused person to examine, at the trial stage, any witness against him with whom he was not confronted during the judicial investigation."[98] In other words, the OCIJ was suggesting that any potential prejudice arising out of the exclusion from the investigative stage could be balanced out or remedied at the trial stage. Unfortunately, as recounted below, once the trial stage was underway, the Court interpreted Rule 84(1) much more narrowly.

Presumption of Admissibility

The procedural approach the Trial Chamber chose for admitting documentary evidence was to grant a broad presumption of admissibility (authenticity and relevance) categorically to a large number of records.[99] The majority of documentary evidence in 002/01 was put before the Chamber in this way. The two largest bodies of documentary evidence granted a presumption of admissibility were (1) documents cited by the OCIJ in the footnotes to the Closing Order and (2) materials provided by the Documentation Center of Cambodia (DC-Cam). It was not clear until several months into the trial that evidence cited in the Closing Order would be granted a presumption of admissibility, but the Trial Chamber made a ruling to this effect in late January of 2012, explaining:

Internal Rule 67(3) requires the Co-Investigating Judges to review and evaluate documents to determine whether as a whole there is sufficient evidence to support the charges against the Accused. It follows that during the judicial investigation, the Co-Investigating Judges assessed all documents placed on the Case File for relevance, and accorded some probative value to the evidence cited in the Closing Order. The Closing Order was subject to appeal to the Pre-Trial Chamber. For these reasons, the Trial Chamber has accorded the documents cited in the Closing Order a presumption of relevance and reliability (including authenticity) and has given them an E3 number.[100]

Three months later, the Chamber made a similar decision about the DC-Cam documents. On the basis of testimony from Youk Chhang and Dara Vanthan, the Trial Chamber deemed, "the methodology used by DC-Cam in obtaining, archiving and preserving contemporaneous DK-era documents to be reliable."[101] Accordingly, the Chamber categorically granted all contemporaneous DK-era documents originating from DC-Cam "a rebuttable presumption of *prima facie* relevance and reliability (including authenticity)."[102] The Court was satisfied that the process for collecting records employed by DC-Cam provided "no reasonable apprehension that documents originating from this source could have been subject to tampering, distortion, or falsification."[103]

The DC-Cam documents, and the presumption of admissibility afforded thereto, are noteworthy because these records represented a very heavy proportion of the documents admitted into evidence that were contemporaneous to the crimes alleged. According to calculations made by the Nuon Chea Defense in their Appeal against the Judgment, approximately 5,800 documents entered into evidence in Case 002/01 and were assigned "E3" numbers (meaning they had been "put before the Chamber" as evidence in Case 002/01). Based on metadata from the Zylab court document management system, the Defense figured that of these 5,800 documents, "approximately 2,000 have DC-Cam numbers, suggesting that is where they originated."[104] Another 1,200 or so were interviews, Civil Party applications, and victim complaints. The remaining 2,600, according to the Defense, "include substantial secondary sources and other non-contemporaneous material."[105] The Defense repeatedly expressed concerns that the Chamber had undertaken inadequate scrutiny of the provenance and reliability of this large body of records.

In the decision granting a rebuttable presumption of authenticity to the DC-Cam records, the Chamber made a point of stating that "the originals" of all DC-Cam documents are retained by the organization, so the Defense "could have requested access to these documents where any genuine concern as to the accuracy of the copy contained on the Case File or as to the provenance or reliability of particular documents existed."[106] This is a curious declaration because, as seen after the testimony, it was in fact not at all clear how many of the one million documents in the DC-Cam archives were truly original documents. When asked to clarify what exactly is meant by "original documents," DC-Cam Director, Youk Chhang, had explained that "[f]or those documents which are not available in Cambodia, they are also considered as original documents."[107] This wording as put forth by the effective custodian of the documents seemed to suggest that DC-Cam was categorizing duplicates of certain documents (photocopies or perhaps microfilm scans) as "original" documents. Youk Chhang also confirmed that during authentication of documents, DC-Cam did not employ any scientific or forensic protocol to examine the documents in order to determine authenticity. He explained that they would typically just look at the color of the paper, date, author, content, and language used in the document for indicia of reliability.[108]

Confrontation Rights of the Accused

In place of oral testimony, and over the strong objections of Defense Counsel, the Chamber also admitted 1,124 written records of interviews with witnesses and Civil Parties who were not called to Court to be examined during the trial. The Nuon Chea Defense argues in its Appeal that only about a third of the statements admitted (about 400) were actually taken by CIJs—the rest were recorded as Civil Party applications or victim complaints by NGOs (like DC-Cam) or individual researcher statements.[109] Here the principal issue wasn't a presumption of authenticity granted to the documents, but rather a violation of the confrontation rights of the Accused. The Chamber justified this decision in reference to expediency, suggesting the right to a speedy trial here trumped the other fair trial rights (like confrontation) that the Defense was seeking to protect:

> As the parties in Case 002 have requested to hear a cumulative total of 1058 witnesses, Civil Parties and experts, it follows that limitation of the right to hear all proposed witnesses, Civil Parties and experts is necessary in order to safeguard the right of the accused to an expeditious trial.[110]

It is difficult not to see merit in Defense arguments about the cumulative prejudicial effect of these procedural decisions with regard to documentary evidence. The relentless focus on expediency as a justification for procedural approaches, at the expense of safeguarding the other rights of the Accused (in particular meaningful confrontation of the evidence) certainly suggests a results-driven process rather than a sincere and objective inquiry into the facts. Whether the cumulative effect of these discretionary decisions amounts to something "so unfair and unreasonable as to constitute an abuse of the Trial Chamber's discretion"[111] is a matter for the Supreme Court Chamber to decide, with the Case 002/01 appeals currently under consideration. But in any event, it is instructive to know the context of the Court's approach to documentary evidence when considering the merit of the conclusions reached in the Judgment.

In the Judgment, the Chamber does address the confrontation concerns of the Defense by assuring the Accused that none of the un-confronted statements would be used for proof of acts and conduct of the Accused, except under certain, narrowly defined circumstances:

> Absent the opportunity for examination, the Chamber excluded statements going to proof of the acts and conduct of the Accused as alleged in the Closing Order. Exceptionally, the Chamber admitted statements going to proof of the Accused's acts and conduct as charged where the witness was deceased, thereby preventing the opportunity for confrontation. For example, TCW-699 died before the close of the hearing, preventing the Chamber from hearing him. Instead the Chamber admitted his prior statement, noting that it would not base any conviction decisively thereupon and thereby safeguarding the rights of the Accused.[112]

The Chamber defends the admission of the large collection of prior statements from non-testifying witnesses on the same grounds: "the statements were relevant to proof of matters other than the acts and conduct of the Accused as charged in the Closing Order, including the historical background, administrative and communications structures, the crime base, Democratic Kampuchea policies, the impact of the crimes on victims and/or the contextual elements of crimes against humanity."[113]

The prohibition against using statements like these to prove the "acts and conduct" of the Accused is supposed to prevent the Court from basing a conviction upon evidence that the Accused was never afforded the right to challenge. But as detailed later in this report in the critical analysis of the Judgment, it seems apparent that the Chamber repeatedly and erroneously relied upon the *de jure* administrative and communications structure of the Khmer Rouge to infer *de facto* control as a basis for convictions under Joint Criminal Enterprise and Superior Responsibility, without any corroborating evidence of the actual "acts and conduct" of the Accused vis-à-vis specific criminal acts.[114] Insofar as the Chamber relied heavily on these un-challenged statements for proof of the administrative and communications structures, and then used their findings about the *de jure* responsibility of the Accused to presume criminal acts and conduct, it is not at all clear how the Court meaningfully protected the confrontation rights of the Accused in this regard.

Barriers to New Evidence

The effect of the broad presumption of admissibility was to usher very large collections of materials into evidence that had come from the investigative stage in the proceedings, (which, as noted above, had more or less excluded the Defense), while at the same time the Court was raising procedural hurdles to hearing and testing other evidence at trial. For example, typically, documents used to confront a witness do not need to be entered into evidence if the sole purpose of the questioning is to impeach the witness, but at the ECCC, the Trial Chamber barred the lawyers from questioning witnesses with any documents that had not been put before the Chamber. It should be noted that this was another area where there was protracted procedural uncertainty, before the bar of this form of confrontation was made clear by the Chamber. Even with documents that were on the Case File and admitted into evidence, trial monitors recorded many objections raised throughout the trial, stemming from the unclear procedures for confronting the persons with documents.[115]

Internal Rule 80(3) provides that the Trial Chamber may order the Parties, "within a prescribed time limit prior to the Initial Hearing," to file certain documents to facilitate efficient trial management, including witness lists, exhibit lists, legal issues they intend to raise at the initial hearing, and a list of new documents and documents already on the Case File which the party seeks to have "put before the Chamber." The Trial Chamber issued such an order in Case 002, prior to severance, and set a deadline of April 2011, six months prior to when the trial would commence.[116] Defense teams objected to the Rule 80 procedure, refused to file document lists so far in advance of trial, and instead filed a series of submissions arguing why this approach to documentary evidence was incompatible with the Cambodian Code of Criminal Procedure (where all evidence is admissible, even until the last day of trial),[117] as well as standard practice in adversarial international criminal tribunals (where accused persons are required to file exhibit lists only after the close of Prosecution evidence).

Although Rule 80 does not state that any document not included in a Party's pre-trial list will be subsequently admissible only if it meets the IR 87(4) requirement that the evidence "was not available before the opening of the trial," the Trial Chamber subsequently made a ruling to this effect.[118] Accordingly, the ECCC placed quite a strict limitation on receipt of "new evidence," pronouncing: "All proposed evidence not available at the time the Chamber is seised with the case is considered 'new' evidence subject to the requirements of Internal Rule 87(4). Parties must demonstrate that new evidence was not available prior to the opening of the trial and/or could not have been discovered earlier with the exercise of reasonable diligence."[119] It should be noted that the Internal Rules were drafted and adopted by the Court to consolidate the applicable procedures from the Cambodian Code of Criminal Procedure along with certain international procedural norms in one guiding instrument.[120] According to the ECCC Law and the UN-Royal Government of Cambodia Agreement, the 2007 Cambodian Code of Criminal Procedure governs ECCC proceedings. Only where there is a lacuna in Cambodian Law (where existing Cambodian procedures are unclear or do not squarely address a unique procedural challenge), or where Cambodian criminal procedure is inconsistent with internationally recognized fair trial standards, is the ECCC meant to seek guidance from international law and practice.[121]

The much less permissive pathway for Rule 87(4) excluded even certain potentially exculpatory evidence from trial. Late in the second year of trial, the Nuon Chea Defense proposed new evidence related to filmmaker Rob Lemkin's work, which it said would be relevant and exculpatory to the alleged policy of targeting Lon Nol soldiers and officials, but the Chamber rejected the submission and refused to summon Lemkin as a witness, on the grounds that the exculpatory film material he allegedly had in his position failed to fulfill the requirements set in IR 87(4) for "new evidence."[122] The Chamber also expressed concern about the amount of time it would add to the proceedings to add this testimony and video evidence.[123]

This refusal to summon a witness appeared to violate the plain language of Rule 84(1). The English version of Rule 84(1) states: "The Accused shall have the absolute right to summon witnesses against him or her whom the Accused had no opportunity to examine during the pre-trial stage."[124] Nevertheless, the Trial Chamber concluded that "absolute" did not mean absolute, in part because this word doesn't appear in the Khmer or French translations of the Rules, and in part because Cambodian law "recognizes the discretion of a presiding judge to decline to hear witnesses whose evidence is considered irrelevant, repetitive of other evidence before the Chamber, or otherwise likely to unnecessarily prolong the proceedings."[125] The Nuon Chea Defense has appealed this decision, commenting:

> It is apparent to the Defence that the Chamber's real reason for declining to seek the original material was not the risk that Lemkin might refuse to cooperate but that he might agree. The Chamber indicated as such: 'considering the frail health of the Accused', Lemkin's cooperation with an investigation might place 'timely delivery of the judgement' at risk. This reasoning is perplexing and disappointing: the Chamber never doubted the likelihood that Lemkin is in possession of exculpatory evidence, and is apparently willing to forgo that evidence in its rush to secure a verdict. It seems that the issuance of a judgment - any judgment - is more important than what that judgment ultimately says.[126]

Responding to the Defense appeals on these issues, the Prosecution has consistently argued that there is no error in law, because the procedural decision the Trial Chamber took in this regard to refuse summonses amounted to a reasonable exercise of discretion.[127] Specifically in regard to the restriction on using documents not in evidence for impeachment purposes only, the Prosecution argued that this procedure had merit because the same prohibition was applied equitably to all the Parties.[128]

Probative Value Assessment?

The general response to all the Defense concerns on documentary evidence was a promise, repeated through the documentary hearing decisions, and articulated again in the Judgment, that of course the Chamber would undertake a careful assessment of probative value of any evidence relied upon in the end.

For instance, the Trial Chamber promised that it would "consider all irregularities in the witnesses' interviews held during the investigative phase as well as all discrepancies between these interviews and their testimony at trial, when determining the probative value and weight to be accorded to the evidence before it."[129] Likewise, Paragraph 34 of the Judgment provides a general recitation of the approach to evaluating probative value of evidence, including the declaration that, "In conjunction with final submissions, the Chamber considers objections to the probative value of evidence made at trial, particularly those that went beyond the *prima facie* relevance and reliability of proposed evidence."[130] However, the rest of the Judgment contains no actual explicit consideration of any Party objections to the probative value of evidence. While Paragraph 34 enumerates "Various factors [that] are relevant to the probative value of evidence,"[131] there are literally only a handful of instances in the rest of the 630-page Judgment where the Trial Chamber demonstrates this weighing of various factors in order to justify reliance on a particular piece of evidence. One is left to simply presume that the Chamber conducted such an analysis, although as will be discussed in Part III of this report, the quality of the factual findings and legal conclusions leave ample basis to doubt such analysis took place.[132]

The Chamber later declares, "the parties availed themselves of these opportunities to make detailed submissions on matters relevant to probative value and thus weight to be assigned to evidence at the conclusion of proceedings. The Chamber considers these submissions and objections in its final assessment of the evidence."[133] But if one reads through the full text of the Judgment, the obvious question that leaps to mind is: *where?* Where in the Judgment does the Chamber consider these submissions or take them into account in its assessment of evidence? This passage in Paragraph 65 is actually one of just eight times the phrase "probative value" even appears in the Judgment at all. Half of these instances are in Paragraphs 34 and 39, where the Chamber expounds upon its general approach to assessing the probative value of evidence. At Paragraph 93, the Chamber quotes a submission by the Khieu Samphan Defense, which had expressed concern that inadequate opportunity for adversarial debate about evidentiary submissions was detrimental to the Defense's ability to make meaningful submissions about the probative value of documentary evidence.[134] Paragraph 397 contains the *sole* instance in the Judgment where the Chamber explicitly articulates an assessment of probative value using that term: "Although Stephen HEDER – whom the Chamber found to be generally credible – testified as to the circumstances in which the interview was conducted, the Chamber has been unable to accord his notes of the interview significant probative value." The Chamber specifies in the corresponding footnote: "In relation to E3/5699, the Chamber has taken into account the fact that no full transcription or recording of the interview was available, the summary of the interview was not signed by VAN Rith, and the interview was conducted informally."[135]

The term "weight" appears exactly 11 times throughout the entire Judgment. Over half of these are in reference to sentencing, declaring how little weight the Chamber decided to afford various behaviors of the Accused as mitigating factors.[136] One instance uses the word weight in its literal sense, in reference to the physical appearance of Khieu Samphan.[137] Another instance occurs in the "Preliminary Issues" section of the Judgment, where the Court refers globally to "the overwhelming weight of the evidence" indicating that the Accused were Khmer Rouge officials between 1975 and 1979.[138] At Paragraph 34, in the section entitled "Evidentiary and Procedural Principles," the Judgment recites the general procedural approach that "Absent the opportunity to examine the source or author of evidence, less weight may be assigned to that evidence."[139] Similarly, Paragraph 66 contains a general statement of principle.[140] As with the phrase "probative value," the *sole* instance where the Judgment uses the word "weight" in the context of an actual explicit assessment of the reliability of a piece of evidence is in Paragraph 397, in regard to the above-mentioned Stephen Heder interview.

A search for other relevant synonyms yields no better results. The word "credible" appears just eight times in the entire Judgment, and the word "credibility" appears six times: twice are in reference to an actual cursory assessment of specific testimonial evidence,[141] while the other instances do not connect with assessing specific evidence.[142] The word "reliability" appears six times, half of which are in reference to actual assessments of specific evidence.[143] The word "reliable" appears just nine times in the entire Judgment—once with respect to a specific piece of documentary evidence,[144] three times to discount the credibility of testimonial evidence that would have been exculpatory,[145] and once to positively assess inculpatory testimonial evidence.[146] The other four instances did not involve assessment of specific evidence.[147]

Reliance on Civil Party Evidence

Concern over the anemic probative value analysis of the Chamber extends beyond the realm of documentary evidence. There was a similarly undiscerning approach to the Chamber's reliance on Civil Party testimony. Over the course of the first segment of Case 002, the Trial Chamber heard testimony from 31 Civil Parties and 58 witnesses. Analysis of the Case 002/01 Judgment reveals a much heavier reliance on Civil Party evidence throughout the Judgment than was the case in the first trial at the ECCC. This supports the declaration of the Civil Parties that they have played a "decisive role" in Case 002/01 in supporting the Prosecution.[148] Despite continued uncertainty over the extent to which the Civil Parties would be fully fledged Parties to the proceedings or have a more limited role, their personal stories have no doubt been heavily employed by the Court in service of the broader narrative produced by the trial process.[149] Over the course of the Case 002/01 proceedings, the Civil Parties provided a range of documentary evidence and oral testimony of relevance to the criminal allegations against the Accused,[150] and first-hand accounts from the Civil Parties have provided a more comprehensive picture of what exactly happened during the forced evacuation from Phnom Penh and subsequent population movements.

Civil Party evidence was cited a total of 787 times in the Case 002/01 Judgment,[151] compared with only 131 times in the Case 001 Judgment.[152] In the Case 001 Judgment, Witnesses were cited more than twice as frequently as Civil Parties in support of factual findings. Comparatively, as table 1 illustrates, the Case 002/01 Judgment revealed a greater relative reliance on Civil Party evidence compared with evidence from Witnesses to support its factual findings.[153] This was despite the fact that in Case 002/01, there were nearly twice as many Witnesses testifying as Civil Parties. Table 1 provides analysis of Civil Party testimony cited, as compared with Witness testimony cited, in the Case 001 and Case 002/01 Judgments. Any comparison between Case 001 and Case 002 must of course be considered in light of the fact that in the former, 238 of the 351 facts alleged against the Accused were admitted by the Defense, and accordingly resulted in a significant proportion of the evidence being comprised of admissions made by the Accused himself.[154]

Table 1. Comparative Reliance on Civil Party Evidence between Case 001 and Case 002/01 Judgment[155]

Case	Testimonial Evidence from Witnesses	Citations in Judgment	Testimonial Evidence from Civil Parties	Citations in Judgment
Case 001	17 fact witnesses/ 7 character witnesses	225 [average per witness: 13.25]	22 Civil Parties	131 [average 5.9 times per Civil Party]
Case 002/01	53 fact witnesses/ 5 character witnesses	1,251 [average per witness: 23.6]	31 Civil Parties	787 [average 25.4 times per Civil Party]

Probative value of Civil Party evidence

The Trial Chamber's reliance on Civil Party evidence in the Case 002/01 Judgment provides positive support for the important role played by the Civil Parties. However, the Trial Chamber's failure to adequately explain how it assessed the probative value of their evidence is problematic. Whether the Trial Chamber should differentiate the probative value of Civil Parties and Witness testimony was a fiercely contested issue throughout the course of the trial. Monitors noted that the Parties, in particular the Ieng Sary and Nuon Chea Defense teams, raised the issue on numerous occasions both in Court and through submissions.[156] The Defense argued that the absence of the threat of perjury engendered by the fact that Civil Parties were not required to take an oath or affirmation prior to providing testimony and the lack of procedural safeguards (compared with ordinary witnesses) renders Civil Party testimony inherently less credible. The Civil Parties, on the other hand, argued that testimony not given under oath is no less probative. In their Closing Brief, the Civil Parties presented arguments in support of the high probative value of Civil Party evidence, arguing that in accordance with the Internal Rules and jurisprudence, the probative value of Civil Party testimony should be assessed in a similar manner to other evidence.[157] Despite numerous requests from the Parties for a clear ruling on the matter, the Chamber never fully addressed the difference between Civil Party and Witness testimony, other than issuing a decision during the evidentiary hearings that stated that the Trial Chamber would determine the probative value of Civil Party testimony on a case-by-case basis in light of its credibility.[158]

Following the Trial Chamber's assurance, the Parties expected that the issue would be resolved in the Case 002/01 Judgment.[159] However, the Judgment not only fails to resolve the lingering question of a distinction between Civil Party and Witness testimony, but also fails to provide any genuine explanation at all for how the Trial Chamber assessed the weight and probative value of either Civil Party or Witness testimony. Part II of the Judgment generally describes the evidentiary and procedural principles that bind the Trial Chamber in its final assessment of the evidence.[160] However, the application of these principles to the evidence relied upon for the factual findings and conclusion is glaringly absent from the analysis. With just a handful of exceptions, references to the probative value of Civil Party and factual Witness testimony used to support conclusions made in relation to the two population movements and Tuol Po Chrey are curiously absent in the analysis.[161] The scarce occasions where the Judgment does mention credibility or probative value are limited to addressing the Khieu Samphan Defense team's objection to the credibility of Witness Phy Phuon (discussed briefly in a footnote), Stephen Heder,[162] and a perfunctory discussion of the credibility of Witness Lim Sat in relation to orders to assemble and kill Lon Nol officials.[163] This is in contrast to the Case 001 Judgment, which demonstrates greater transparency in the analysis of factors relevant to the credibility of and weight afforded to Witness and Civil Party evidence.[164]

Use of victim impact statements/statements of suffering

A further issue concerning Civil Party evidence in the Judgment is the Trial Chamber's use of victim impact statements or statements of suffering, to support its factual findings relevant to guilt. The statements of suffering allowed a number of Civil Parties to provide oral evidence on their suffering over four trial days in May-June 2013. During the trial, the Chamber had confirmed on a number of occasions with the Parties that the sole purpose of the victim impact statements was to determine matters relevant to reparations and sentencing. The Chamber assured the Defense that the statements would not be relevant to establishing the guilt of the Accused. Since the evidence provided by Civil Parties would not be relied on to support factual findings relevant to guilt, the Defense teams were only permitted to comment on the statements after the Civil Party had left the courtroom. However, despite the assurances provided by the Chamber, the Case 002/01 Judgment refers to evidence provided during the victim impact statements on multiple occasions in the Judgment to support factual findings relevant to the liability of the Accused. As discussed in more detail in Part III of this report, this denied the Defense an opportunity to confront consequential evidence used to establish the guilt of the Accused.[165]

CIVIL PARTY ENGAGEMENT

Another aspect of the trial that remained in flux throughout Case 002/01, and gave rise to consequential procedural uncertainties for the Parties, was the mechanism for Civil Party engagement. As noted in the introduction, a number of changes have been made to the Civil Party participation scheme since the first version of the Internal Rules were adopted at the judicial plenary session on 12 June 2007.[166] Before we can examine the Civil Party engagement in Case 002/01, it is important to recount the changes made to the victim participation scheme from Case 001 to Case 002/01, including amendments to the Internal Rules and a comparative assessment of procedural rulings and decisions relevant to Civil Party participation. After laying this foundation, the following section offers critical assessment of how the changes affected the actual participation of the Civil Parties during the trial. In particular, the report considers whether the changes resulted in increased efficiency during proceedings in Case 002/01—a primary impetus for the modified system. Moreover, the report will also reflect on the Plenary's claim that the modifications would "enhance the quality of Civil Party representation" while allowing the Trial Chamber to effectively "balance the rights of all Parties."[167]

Drawing on over five years of monitoring the proceedings at the ECCC, this section of the report uses data gathered by the Asian International Justice Initiative's (AIJI) Khmer Rouge Tribunal (KRT) monitoring team over 22 weeks of proceedings in Case 001 and 67 weeks in Case 002/01.[168] Monitors have documented, analyzed, and reported on all issues, including victim participation from the commencement of the Initial Hearings in both trials through to release of the final verdict. Using this analysis, this section of the report draws comparisons between the procedural frameworks for victim participation adopted in Case 001 and Case 002/01, and how victims actually participated in the proceedings. Although monitors have noted that other factors also impacted participation, it is nonetheless useful to compare and contrast the victim participation scheme adopted in Case 001 and Case 002/01 in terms of the quality and quantity of victim representation and trial efficiency.[169]

Structural Changes to the Victim Participation Scheme

The final changes to the victim participation scheme that was to apply during Case 001 were agreed on during the 5th Plenary session in March 2009, just before Case 001 went to trial.[170] The amendments required Civil Parties to be represented by a lawyer and determined that although they could still exercise rights as Parties to the proceedings, they could only participate through their lawyers.[171] Accordingly, at the commencement of hearings in Case 001, Civil Parties had the right to:

- Participate in criminal proceedings against those responsible for crimes within the jurisdiction of the ECCC by supporting the Prosecution;
- Seek collective and moral reparations.[172]

As noted by monitors in the final report on Case 001, a lack of specific guidance in the Internal Rules left the Trial Chamber with broad discretion to interpret the role of the Civil Parties as the trial progressed. Rather than clearly defining rules of participation from the outset, the Trial Chamber generally exercised its discretion in a reactive and unpredictable manner, leaving the Civil Parties and their lawyers in a constant state of uncertainty as to their role in the courtroom.[173]

In September 2009, just before the conclusion of evidentiary hearings for Case 001, judicial officers at the 6th Plenary session agreed on significant modifications to the Civil Party participation scheme moving forward to a trial in Case 002.[174] By this stage, thousands of Civil Parties had filed applications for Civil Party status in Case 002. With such a large number of Civil Parties likely to participate in the next trial, the system employed during Case 001 was considered to be unfeasible. It was generally accepted by all the Parties that some change was required to ensure the expedience of the trial.[175] In its final report critically assessing victim participation in the first case before the ECCC, the Asian International Justice Initiative trial monitoring group agreed that a more coordinated and clear approach to Civil Party representation was necessary in order to serve the interests of victims. However, trial monitors also noted that the Court had, in focusing on trial efficiency, not paid sufficient attention to the qualitative aspects of victim participation. In preparation for Case 002, they further recommended that the Trial Chamber issue a practice direction clearly delineating the role of Civil Party Lawyers (CPLs) supported by appropriate Civil Law or international jurisprudence in addition to factors related to expediency.[176]

New rules adopted in 2010 at the 7th Plenary determined that Civil Parties would no longer participate individually in the proceedings at the trial stage. Instead, after the Pre-Trial phase, the Civil Parties would form a "consolidated group," represented by two lawyers—one National and one International Lead Co-Lawyer for Civil Parties. The new Civil Party Lead Co-Lawyers (CPLCLs) Section of the Court was given responsibility to coordinate the CPLs in terms of advocacy, strategy, and in-court representation. Together, the two lawyers were entrusted to represent the interests of the entire consolidated group. However, since the CPLs still maintained direct contact with their clients and power of attorney, the workability of the new system appeared to rely on the extent to which the CPLCLs and the CPLs could work effectively together to reach consensus.

The new scheme also included a change to the timing of admissibility claims for Civil Party applications from the Trial phase to the Pre-Trial phase.[177] This change avoided the problematic situation in Case 001 where the Trial Chamber heard challenges to the admissibility of Civil Parties during the trial itself—notably after they had participated in over seven months of evidentiary hearings.[178] The positive effects of the change were twofold. Firstly, it meant that trial time was not required to hear admissibility claims. Secondly, it avoided the disappointment and uncertainty inherent in allowing Civil Parties to participate in the trial when they faced the prospect of being found inadmissible at the conclusion.[179] During the 8th Plenary, further amendments were introduced, including an avenue for Civil Parties to seek reparations via external third-party funding in addition to the Accused or convicted-borne forms of reparation that existed before. This provided an additional avenue to seek reparations where an accused person is found to be indigent.[180]

Accordingly, at the start of proceedings in Case 002, the Civil Parties faced a new modified scheme of participation, which limited their direct participation in the proceedings through the formation of a consolidated group. Although the new framework resolved some of the most prominent issues related to the participation of victims during the first trial—namely, the determination of Civil Party admissibility prior to the commencement of the trial and the inclusion of non-judicial measures for reparations—it also created new uncertainties regarding the role victims would play in the second trial against the alleged Senior Leaders of Democratic Kampuchea.

Table 2 summarizes the key changes to the victim participation scheme limited to admissibility and legal representation, as reflected in the Internal Rules as amended from Case 001 to Case 002/01.

Given that the Civil Party provisions in the amended Internal Rules had not yet been interpreted by the Court, the Civil Parties approached the second trial at the ECCC in much the same way as they had approached the first trial—asserting robust rights as fully fledged Parties to the proceedings. As discussed above, a lack of specific guidance in the Internal Rules on exactly how the Civil Parties would participate in the trial left the Trial Chamber with broad discretion to determine the role the Civil Parties and their lawyers would play. Trial monitors noted that this was determined largely by the exigencies of the trial.[181] During the course of the trial in Case 001, the Trial Chamber gradually chipped away at the notion that the Civil Parties would participate on equal terms with the other Parties, as it struggled to deal with both the practicalities of their involvement during the trial and to balance their role with the rights of the Accused.

Despite significant changes to the victim participation scheme, channeling the voices of the Civil Parties through the auspice of the CPLCLs Section, there was little change to the procedural rights extended to the Civil Parties by the Trial Chamber during the hearings for Case 001 and Case 002/01. Early on in Case 001, the Trial Chamber ruled that the Civil Parties would not be permitted to make opening statements, pose questions on the character of the Accused, or make submissions on sentencing.[182] This position was maintained during the second trial. Table 3 compares how the procedural rights exercised by the Civil Parties either through Counsel or through the CPLCLs changed from Case 001 to Case 002/01, as determined by various rulings and decisions of the Trial Chamber.

Given that the procedural rights of the Civil Parties had already been limited in the early stages of Case 001, and were substantially the same across the two evidentiary hearings, the fundamental shift in the in-court representation of the Civil Parties between Case 001 and Case 002/01 was the consolidation of legal representation of the Civil Parties through the CPLCLs.[183] A further change in the way victims participated in the trial from Case 001 to Case 002/01 is reflected in the Trial Chamber's decision in late 2012 to allow the Civil Parties to "speak on the totality of [the] suffering [they] experienced during the DK period" at the conclusion of their statements. These were commonly referred to as "victim impact hearings," and in an effort to reduce the psychological stress imposed on the Civil Party, the Chamber prohibited the Defense from commenting on the statements until after the Civil Party had left the courtroom. Rather than reflecting any fundamental shift in procedural rights afforded to Civil Parties at

Table 2: Amendments to the Internal Rules Impacting Victim Participation, Comparing Case 001 with Case 002/01

Procedure	Case 001[184]	Case 002/01[185]
Deadline for application to participate as a Civil Party	Rule 23(4): 10 days prior to Initial Hearing.	Rule *23bis* (2): A Victim who wishes to be joined as a Civil Party shall submit such application in writing no later than fifteen (15) days after the Co-Investigating Judges notify the parties of the conclusion of the judicial investigation.
Admissibility criteria	Rule 23(2): The right to take civil action may be exercised by Victims of a crime coming within the jurisdiction of the ECCC.	Rule 23*bis*: The Civil Party applicant shall ... demonstrate as a direct consequence of at least one of the crimes alleged against the Charged Person, that he or she in fact suffered physical, material or psychological injury.
Decision on admissibility	Rule 100: The Chamber shall [...] rule on the admissibility and the substance of such claims against the Accused.	Rule 100: OCIJ decides on Civil Party applications on or before issue of Closing Order.
Appeal of decision on admissibility	Rule 103(2): The Judgment is open to appeal. The time limits for appeal shall commence from the date of the Judgment, or notification, as appropriate. Rule 107, which governs time limits for appeals to the SCC: Appeals against decisions of the Trial Chamber must be filed within 30 days of the date of judgment, or of its notification, as appropriate.	Rule 74(4) allows Civil Parties to appeal against specific orders by the OCIJ, including declaring a Civil Party application inadmissible, among others. Rule 77*bis* expedites appeals to the Pre-Trial Chamber regarding the admissibility of Civil Party applications, on the basis of written submissions alone that must be filed within 10 days of notification of the OCIJ decision on admissibility. Any response shall be filed within 5 days of notification of the appeal of the other party. The decision of the Pre-Trial Chamber (PTC) shall be final.
Determination of Civil Party claims	Rule 100: The Chamber shall make a decision on any Civil Party claims in the Judgment.	Rule 100: The Chamber shall make a decision on any Civil Party claims in the Judgment. The Chamber shall not hand down Judgment on the Civil Party action that is in contradiction with the Judgment on the criminal action in the same case.
Legal representation	Rule 12(2)(g): The Victims Unit shall facilitate the participation of Victims and the common representation of Civil Parties. Rule 23(7): Any Victim participating in proceedings before the ECCC as a Civil Party has the right to be represented by a national lawyer, or a foreign lawyer in collaboration with a national lawyer. Rule 23(8): A group of Civil Parties may choose to be represented by a common lawyer drawn from the list held by the Victims Unit.	Rule *12ter*: CPLCLs section shall ensure the effective organization of Civil Party representation during the trial stage and beyond. Shall first and foremost seek the views of the CPLs and endeavor to reach consensus in order to coordinate representation of Civil Parties at trial. Internal procedures developed by the CPLCLs in consultation with the CPLs. Core functions: 1) Represent the interests of the consolidated group of Civil Parties and act as their advocate in court presentations; 2) Provide strategy to this group during the trial stage and beyond. 3) CPLs shall endeavor to support the CPLCLs in the representation of the interests of the consolidated group. Support shall be mutually agreed between the CPLCLs and CPLs.

Table 3. Procedural Rights of Civil Parties, Comparing Case 001 with Case 002/01

Procedural right	Case 001	Case 002/01
Participation in hearings on appeals against provisional detention orders	N/A[186]	Permitted (limited to brief oral observations)[187]
Opening statements	Not permitted[188]	Not permitted[189]
Questions on the character of the Accused	Not permitted[190]	Not permitted[191]
Questions directly from Civil Parties to the Accused	Permitted (through President)[192]	Permitted (through President)[193]
Submissions on sentencing	Not permitted[194]	Not permitted[195]
Statement of suffering/harm	Limited to facts and subject to Defense examination[196]	Not limited to facts and not subject to Defense examination[197]
In-court representation	Directed through Civil Party Lawyers[198]	Questions coordinated by Lead Co-Lawyers on behalf of consolidated group[199]

trial, the change from Case 001 to Case 002/01 appeared to reflect a response to the difficulties posed by the Trial Chamber's own Severance Order, which *prima facie* compelled Civil Parties to compartmentalize the harm they suffered in order to fit within the facts of the severed case.[200]

Impact of Structural Changes to the Victim Participation Scheme on Meaningful Representation, Civil Party Participation, and Trial Efficiency

The amalgamation of the Civil Parties into one consolidated group raised a number of questions concerning the extent to which this would affect the meaningful participation of victims. CPLs voiced concerns that the creation of the CPLCLs Section would limit the scope of reparations victim groups could seek, and potentially dilute the representation of diverse interests among the Civil Parties. Considering that changes to the victim participation scheme were intended to result in improved efficiency and "enhanced civil party participation," it is pertinent to consider whether this goal was achieved. Although the significant increase in numbers of Civil Parties in Case 002/01 rendered it practically impossible to hear a similarly large proportion of the victims as Case 001, it is nonetheless important to critique the aspiration-versus-reality of the Civil Party complaint mechanism in terms of it being considered an avenue for direct victim participation in the trial process. To conduct this analysis, both the quantitative and qualitative aspects of changes to Civil Party representation have been considered between the two trials.

Representation of victims
Overall, the number of Civil Parties increased significantly from Case 001 to Case 002/01. However, the proportion of Civil Parties that were heard during the trial actually decreased, along with the amount of time used by the CPLs compared to the other Parties. Table 4 compares the total estimated number of victims in relation to the case, the number of applications for Civil Party status, the number finally declared admissible, and the number of Civil Parties who provided testimony during the trial.

Table 4. Victim Representation from Case 001 to Case 002/01

	Total estimated victims[201]	Civil Party applications	Initially declared admissible [202]	Declared admissible (on appeal)[203]	Provided *viva voce* testimony	Percentage [204]
Case 001	>12, 000	94	66	76[205]	22[206]	29%
Case 002/01	1.7-2.2 million	3,988	2,123	3,869[207]	31	<1%

From Case 001 to Case 002/01, there was a significant reduction in the proportion of Civil Parties who were able to participate in the trial by providing oral testimony. While 29 percent of Civil Parties who admitted in Case 001 were able to give testimony during the trial, less than 1 percent of admitted Civil Parties provided testimony during the proceedings for Case 002/01. Allowing a similar proportion of Civil Parties to give evidence in Case 002/01 as had appeared in the first trial was practically unfeasible, since it would have required hearing testimony from more than 1,000 Civil Parties. However, it is important to consider that, paradoxically, despite the larger and more representative number of Civil Parties admitted in Case 002/01 as compared with Case 001, proportionately their voices were less represented at the trial stage.[208]

One noteworthy positive improvement to Civil Party participation from Case 001 to Case 002/01 was the increased level of attendance by the Civil Parties at trial hearings. Monitors noted that during Case 001, the limited availability of resources meant that many Civil Parties were not financially able to attend the hearings, so seats allocated to Civil Parties in the courtroom remained empty for most of the trial.[209] The situation improved markedly during Case 002/01. Approximately 30 Civil Parties attended the proceedings daily—either in the courtroom or in the public gallery.[210]

Trial time utilized by Civil Parties versus the other Parties

Despite obvious differences in the scope and complexity of the second trial, in terms of assessing quantitative representation, it is nonetheless instructive to consider the proportion of trial time utilized by the Civil Parties during both trials vis-à-vis the other Parties. Since the impetus for the consolidation of the Civil Parties was fuelled by criticism that Civil Parties had been "cumbersome" and had lengthened the proceedings in Case 001, it is interesting to see whether the new system actually resulted in a more streamlined process in terms of trial efficiency.[211] Figure 1 sets out the total number of hours utilized by each of the Parties during the evidentiary hearings and reveals a significant reduction in the proportion of time used by the Civil Parties compared to other Parties from Case 001 to Case 002/01.

During Case 001, the Civil Parties utilized almost 42 percent of the total time used by all Parties. During Case 002/01, the relative proportion of time they used dropped to just 15 percent. Table 4 shows a significant shift in the relative proportion of time utilized by Parties—particularly in relation to the Civil Parties. The slightly higher proportion of time used by the Prosecution vis-à-vis the Defense in Case 001 was also mirrored in Case 002/01.[212] Changes between the Parties' relative use of time during the two cases suggest that the Trial Chamber maintained largely the same approach to the Defense's and

Figure 1. Proportional Trial Time Utilized by the Parties in Case 002/01

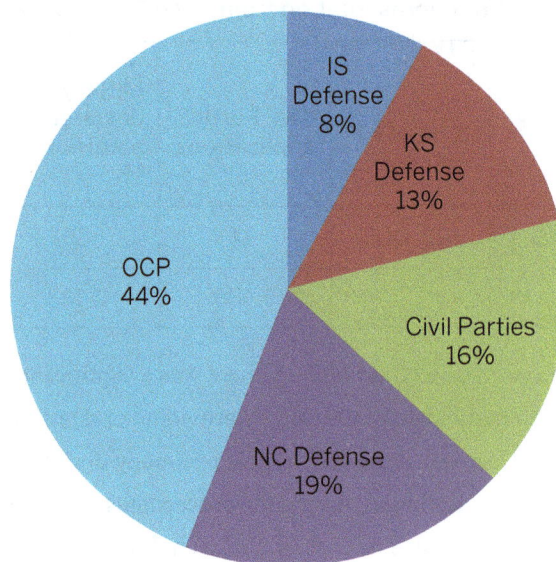

Source: Table 5

Prosecution's use of time adopted in Case 001, despite the increased number of Defense teams in the second case. In relation to the Civil Parties' use of time, as table 5 clearly shows, the consolidation of the Civil Parties led to an overall reduction in the use of time from Case 001 to Case 002/01.

Despite a clear reduction in the time dedicated to Civil Party participation, it is difficult to determine whether the consolidation actually resulted in greater efficiency, and/or whether the Trial Chamber simply reduced the time allocations for Civil Party representation compared to the other parties—something that could have also been achieved under the previous system. Particularly when the new scheme was presented to the Parties as an approach that would "greatly enhance meaningful Civil Party participation" in Case 002, it is difficult to see how this was achieved when the overall percentage of victims represented in Court and the proportion of time allocated to their lawyers were reduced.[213] Moreover, as discussed throughout this report, many other factors contributed to inefficiency during the trial, which should also be taken into account when considering the extent to which the role of the Civil Parties impacted the efficiency of the trial.[214] There did, however, appear to be a reduction in allegations of repetitive questions posed by the CPLs between Case 001 and Case 002/01. Trial monitors documented repetitive questions as a significant issue affecting proceedings seven times over the evidentiary hearings in Case 002/01; however, only one of these occasions concerned questioning by a Civil Party Lawyer.[215]

Participation of Civil Party Lawyers alongside Lead Co-Lawyers

Trial monitors observed that a fairly representative sampling of CPLs participated throughout the hearings for Case 002/01, as at least one lawyer from each of the 12 groups addressed the Court during the Case 002/01 proceedings. Analysis of the in-court representation of Civil Parties during Case 002/01 reveals that the CPLs, rather than the CPLCLs, undertook the majority of questioning of all witnesses, Civil Parties, and experts who provided testimony before the Trial Chamber over the course of Case 002/01. Although the CPLCLs played a prominent role during the trial, speaking on issues concerning the consolidated group as a whole, they generally handed over to the CPLs the responsibility of questioning

Table 5. Breakdown of Time Utilized by Parties, Comparing Case 001 with Case 002/01[216]

Case		Defense			OCPU	Civil Parties
Case 001	Trial Day Time Utilized (Hours/Minutes)	46h 38m			51h 8m	70h 30m
	Percentage of Total Time Utilized Compared with Other Parties	27.71%			30.4%	41.9%
Case 002/01	Trial Day Time Utilized (Hours/Minutes)	Total (all teams) 304h 53m			325h 16m	115h 13m
		IS 62h 34m	NC 42h 19m	KS 99h 59m		
	Percentage of Total Time Utilized Compared with Other Parties	8.0%	19.1%	13.4%	43.6%	15.5%
		40.9%				

their own clients and speaking on specific issues of particular relevance to the sub-groups of Civil Parties they represented. Table 6 shows the proportion of witnesses, experts, and Civil Parties who were questioned by CPLs, the CPLCLs, or a combination of both during the Case 002/01 proceedings.[217]

Either CPLs or CPLCLs were able to put questions to 88 percent of all individuals who provided evidence before the Trial Chamber. All 31 Civil Parties who provided testimony before the Trial Chamber were questioned by at least one Civil Party Lawyer. In five of these cases, the CPLCLs posed additional questions to the Civil Party. Of the 10 individuals who were questioned solely by either Lead-Co Lawyer Pich Ang or Elisabeth Simonneau-Fort, nine were witnesses, and the other was expert Chhim Sotheara.[218]

Representation of victims

In a qualitative sense, it is difficult to assess whether the consolidation of the Civil Parties into a single group under the coordination of the CPLCLs resulted in any enhancement to the meaningful participation at the trial stage of victims in Case 002. During Case 001, Civil Parties exercised a form of direct participation in the proceedings through their respective lawyers. Throughout the course of Case 001, Civil Party Lawyers were able to make independent submissions to the Court. During the hearings, they were also permitted to question witnesses, experts, and Civil Parties on issues that related specifically to the harm suffered by their individual clients, rather than the consolidated group. In June 2009, following frustrations with what appeared to be repetitive or irrelevant questions from the CPLs during the hearings, and at the behest of the Trial Chamber, the CPLs began to direct questions through two representatives

Table 6. Questioning of Witnesses, Experts, and Civil Parties by Civil Party Lawyers and Civil Party Co-Lawyers[219]

Total Number of Witnesses, Experts, and Civil Parties Testifying in 002/01	Questioned by Both Lead Co-Lawyers and Civil Party Lawyers[220]	Questioned Only by Civil Party Lawyers[221]	Questioned Only by Lead Co-Lawyers[222]	Time Voluntarily Allocated to OCP[223]
92	23	58	16	1
Number Questioned as a Percentage of the Total	25%	63%	11%	1%

selected to represent the entire group. Monitors noted that after this time, the self-selecting system appeared to function effectively despite the absence of any coordinating body or mechanism.[224]

Following the creation of the CPLCLs, the CPLs maintained their attorney-client relationship with the Civil Parties at the ECCC, but the two Lead Co-Lawyers had ultimate authority over issues related to trial strategy. During the evidentiary hearings, instead of each Civil Party Lawyer questioning witnesses, Civil Parties, and experts, the Internal Rules required the CPLCLs to coordinate questions on behalf of the consolidated group. Individual submissions were no longer permitted. All filings were required to be submitted to the Court through the section. Because the CPLCLs were appointed by the Court, rather than nominated by the CPLs, they could exercise much more decisive authority over the group of CPLs by, for instance, refusing to put forward a filing from an individual CPL. Accordingly, the only avenue for CPLs to voice disagreement with a filing agreed by the CPLCLs was to request that their name be removed from the filing. This was noted to have occurred in relation to CPL Silke Studzinsky's attempt to file submissions on behalf of her clients that had been rejected by the CPLCLs.[225]

Despite being consolidated into a single group, CPLs represent clients with diverse interests, having been admitted on the basis of distinct and specific harms. The CPLs too come from different legal traditions, bringing with them different and potentially conflicting approaches to trial strategy. To manage disagreements between the CPLs, in August 2011, the CPLCLs adopted internal regulations intended to facilitate coordination amongst the consolidated group.[226] As these regulations and internal meetings between the CPLCLs and the Civil Parties are confidential, analysis of how the new system functioned internally is limited to observations made during the hearings in Case 002/01 and documents on the public record. Whether and how disagreements between both the CPLCLs and the CPLs were resolved, and the effectiveness of the mechanisms governing the consolidated group, is an area for further discussion, but is beyond the scope of this report.

Civil Parties Claims in the Case 002/01 Judgment

The Case 002/01 Judgment is the first decision to consider Civil Party requests for reparation under the modified reparations scheme. Following the Trial Chamber's rejection of the majority of reparations requests made in Case 001, it was hoped that the new scheme would provide greater flexibility and ultimately better outcomes for the Civil Parties should a guilty verdict be found. Although the decision ultimately endorsed the majority of reparations projects sought by the Civil Parties in Case 002/01, the Judgment raises serious concerns over a lack of transparency in the Trial Chamber's approach to Civil

Party participation. In particular, it will describe the transformation of the reparations scheme from Case 001 to Case 002, and reflect on how the Trial Chamber determined the reparations awards within the modified framework. The impact of the Severance Order on the Civil Parties' right to reparations will also be considered as a factor that has shaped the claimant-driven process.

Civil Party reparations scheme

The reparations scheme underwent significant change between Case 001 and 002.[227] During the first trial, the Trial Chamber was limited to awarding collective and moral reparations enforceable against and borne by the Accused. In Case 002/01, the system was modified in two major ways. Firstly, reparations claims were to be submitted as a single claim on behalf of the consolidated group of Civil Parties. Secondly, the amendments introduced an additional avenue for implementation of the awards, in addition to the award against the convicted person—namely, they allow awards to be funded by an external third party. The Victim Support Section's mandate was also expanded to assist the CPLCLs to secure sufficient funds for reparations projects and to develop and implement non-judicial programs. Accordingly, the procedural framework that applied in Case 002/01 allowed the Trial Chamber to award collective and moral reparations that:

- acknowledge the harm suffered by Civil Parties as a result of the commission of the crimes for which an Accused is convicted;
- provide benefits to the Civil Parties which address this harm.

In relation to the harm suffered, the consolidated reparations request was required to contain a reasoned argument as to how the reparations address the harm suffered and reference if the award relates to a specific Civil Party group within the larger group. The major changes to the reparations scheme from Case 001 to Case 002/01 are described in table 7.

Specific reparations awards

In Case 001, the Trial Chamber rejected over 90 percent of the Civil Party requests on the basis that they could not be awarded against Duch either due to the determination of indigence, the request was not sufficiently specified, or because the implementation was beyond the jurisdiction of the ECCC.[228] Accordingly, reparations awards in the first trial were limited to the compilation of apologies made by Duch during the trial and publication of the names of the Civil Parties in the Judgment. Following reparations requests via external third-party funding, the Trial Chamber endorsed 11 of the 13 reparations projects submitted by the CPLCLs. The two projects that were rejected by the Court had not demonstrated that they had secured sufficient external funding to satisfy the implementation requirement.[229] Since all 11 reparations projects awarded had been externally funded and many had already been implemented at the time the Judgment was delivered, the Trial Chamber's endorsement was considered by some to be a "rubber-stamping" exercise.[230] Further analysis of the extent to which the Trial Chamber responded effectively to the Civil Parties' submissions in relation to reparations is limited by the fact that at the time the Judgment was issued (and even at the time of writing this report) the Civil Parties' final request for reparations was only available in the French and Khmer language.[231]

Trial Chamber findings on harm suffered by the Civil Parties

The Case 002/01 Judgment's findings on harm can be loosely divided into three sections: an assessment of the harm suffered by Civil Parties, a finding that the suffering was a result of the crimes committed by the Accused, and a determination as to the 13 reparations submitted to the Court intended to address the harm.

Table 7. Amendments to Victim Participation: Internal Rules from Case 001 to Case 002/01

Procedure	Case 001[232]	Case 002/01[233]

Reparations scheme	Rule 23(11):
	
	Subject to Article 39 of the ECCC Law, the Chambers may award only collective and moral reparations to Civil Parties. These shall be awarded against, and be borne by convicted persons.
	
	(12) Such awards may take the following forms:
	
	a) An order to publish the judgment in any appropriate news or other media at the convicted person's expense:
	
	b) An order to fund any non-profit activity or service that is intended for the benefit of Victims; or
	
	c) Other appropriate and comparable forms of reparation.
		Rule 23*quinquies*:
		
		(1): If an Accused is convicted, the Chambers may award only collective and moral reparations to Civil Parties.
		
		(2): Reparations shall be requested in a single submission, which may seek a limited number of awards. The submission shall provide:
		
		  a) a description of the awards sought;
		  b) reasoned argument as to how they address the harm suffered and specify, where applicable, the Civil Party group within the consolidated group to which they pertain; and
		  c) in relation to each award, the single, specific mode of implementation described in Rule 23*quinquies*(3)(a)-(b) sought.
		
		(3): In deciding the modes of implementation of the awards, the Chamber may, in respect of each award, either:
		
		  a) order that the costs of the award shall be borne by the convicted person; or
		  b) recognize that a specific project appropriately gives effect to the award sought by the CPLCLs and may be implemented. Such project shall have been designed or identified in cooperation with the Victim Support Section (VSS) and have secured sufficient external funding.
		
		Rule 80*bis*:
		
		(4): The Trial Chamber may direct the Lead Co-Lawyers, within a deadline determined by the Chamber, to provide initial specification of the substance of the awards they intend to seek within the final claim for collective and moral reparation pursuant to Rule 23*quinquies*(3)(b). At a later stage, the Chamber will determine the date by which the Lead Co-Lawyers shall file the final claim for collective and moral reparation.
		
		(5): The final claim for collective and moral reparation may deviate from the initial specification where necessary, but shall in any case specify both the substance and the mode of implementation of each award.

Non-judicial measures	N/A	Rule 12 *bis*: (3): The Victims Support Section shall be entrusted with the development and implementation of non-judicial programs and measures addressing the broader interests of victims.

The Trial Chamber Judges confirmed the requirement that the harm suffered by Civil Parties must be as a result of the crimes against humanity committed by Nuon Chea and Khieu Samphan during the population movements and executions at Tuol Po Chrey. [234] Referring to the 31 Civil Parties who provided factual testimony and victim impact statements during the course of Case 002/01, the Trial Chamber broadly defined the harms to include psychological suffering, economic loss, loss of dignity, psychological trauma, and grief arising from the loss of family members and relations.[235]

Approaching the question of whether the reparations projects put forward by the CPLCL provided benefits to the Civil Parties that address the harms described above appears to be limited to those Civil Parties that appeared before the Court and Civil Party submissions included in the final claim for reparations. Although the Judgment determined that all 13 reparations projects "may well have addressed the harms suffered" and went beyond the individuals admitted as Civil Parties to the broader victim population, the extent to which the Trial Chamber engaged in a systematic assessment of harm is uncertain.[236] The Judgment states that the Chamber had "regard" to other Civil Party applications on the Case File; however, no citations are provided to specify whether and how this was done.[237] References to the reparations mechanism as "claimant-driven" in the Case 001 Judgment suggest that submissions from the Civil Parties appropriately form the basis of reparations determinations.[238] However, as stated above, any analysis of the extent to which the Trial Chamber relied on the description of harm submitted by the CPLCLs in its final claim for reparations is limited by the existence of only French and Khmer language versions of the filing.

Impact of the Severance Order on Civil Party reparations

The extent to which the Trial Chamber's decision to sever the proceedings impacted the Civil Parties claim for reparations has been a major issue for the Civil Parties during Case 002/01. The concern was that only some Civil Parties—those who could prove a link between the harm suffered and the crimes covered in the first segment of the trial—would be able to seek reparations as a result of the Severance Order.[239] Consistent with the Trial Chamber's findings in the Case 001 Judgment, that the harm must be "directly attributable to the crimes for which the Accused is convicted,"[240] the CPLCL proceeded on the basis that only those Civil Parties who were admitted in relation to Case 002/01 would have legal standing in the trial.[241] The CPLCLs calculated that this included 750 of the total 3,989 Civil Parties admitted in Case 002 who had suffered harm related to the crimes covered by the severed Case 002/01. Although the Trial Chamber informed the CPLCLs that the Severance Order would not limit the Civil Parties' right to moral and collective reparations, their request for clarification on the legal standing of these Civil Parties as a result of the severance was never fully addressed.[242] In February 2012, in its decision on the Appeal for Case 001, the Supreme Court Chamber departed from the approach taken by the Trial Chamber by preferring an interpretation that privileged "the most inclusive measures of reparation."[243] The Trial Chamber continued to assure the Civil Parties that the severance would not affect them, but declined to address the underlying issue.

The Case 002/01 Judgment briefly considers the impact of the Severance Order on the Civil Party claims for reparations—reiterating its position that "the severance of charges will place no limitation on the ability of individual members of the consolidated group to benefit from any reparations ultimately endorsed or awarded by the Trial Chamber."[244] However, clarification on how the severance affected the legal standing of those Civil Parties excluded from the first segment of the trial—an ongoing concern for the Civil Parties throughout the trial—is patently absent from the analysis. This issue is particularly apparent in the endorsement of Project 13, which obliged the Trial Chamber to identify those Civil Parties that would be listed on the ECCC website in relation to Case 002/01. The Case 002/01 Judgment annexes the names of all Civil Parties who participated in Case 002, despite the fact that many of them have suffered harm unrelated to the commission of the crimes for which Khieu Samphan and Nuon Chea were convicted.

Although the position adopted by the Trial Chamber appears to be consistent with the Supreme Court Chamber's view that reparations should be interpreted broadly to include all victims, this may provide additional challenges to the formulation of reparations projects in Case 002/02. The harms suffered by Civil Parties as a consequence of the crimes of genocide, rape, and forced marriage which will be adjudicated in Case 002/02 are likely to be more specific, affecting minority sub-groups within the larger consolidated group. Accordingly, the CPLCLs may find it difficult to prioritize projects that address those specific harms, while also ensuring that reparations provide benefits to all the Civil Parties generally.

Part III: Critical Analysis of the Judgment

A well-reasoned final Judgment in an international criminal trial can be a powerful tool in important respects. A well-reasoned opinion provides a clear and verifiable record of what happened, how it happened, who was responsible, and, at times, an account of why they acted as they did. A trial is supposed to seek truth through a rigorous process of investigation, advocacy, objective assessment, and unbiased application of law to the facts based upon exhaustive weighing of competing evidence and arguments. If a tribunal can faithfully execute this process, it may provide some new insight to the broader historical understanding about a fiercely contested period of violent conflict, thus contributing to processes of reconciliation and of education of future generations. A well-reasoned legal opinion as expressed in a final written decision is also a matter of fairness and due process. All Parties to a criminal proceeding deserve a clear and straightforward articulation of the disposition of the Chamber on all charges, and the reasons and justifications for the factual findings and legal conclusions. Reasoned opinions are fundamental in protecting a meaningful right of appeal.[245] An ill-organized, confusing, or poorly reasoned Judgment only creates difficulties for the Parties and the appellate body. Finally, there is the matter of precedential and jurisprudential value of the Judgment. The international criminal justice "system," such as it is, is still evolving, largely through the case law of the various international and hybrid criminal tribunals. The body of jurisprudence is relatively small but growing, and the Judgment of one tribunal, well-reasoned or not, will certainly have ripple effects that affect subsequent decisions in other tribunals. Above all, however, it is a fundamental obligation of judges in international criminal proceedings to meet the highest standards and best practices in the writing of well-reasoned and logically grounded final judgments, on which not only the liberty of accused individuals depends, but to some extent the history and the future of post-conflict societies rests.

Unfortunately, the Judgment in Case 002/01 provides limited insight, raises concerns about fair trial rights, and should be viewed with caution by anyone seeking to rely upon it as a persuasive piece of jurisprudence in another criminal case. It does not, in our view, meet the requisite standards of international practice, as seen, for example, in the writing of final Judgments at the International Criminal Tribunal for the former Yugoslavia (ICTY) and the permanent International Criminal Court (ICC). Bearing in mind the many procedural issues surveyed in the previous section, we now turn our attention to a detailed analysis of the Judgment that the trial produced. This section begins by critiquing the form and organization of the Judgment, followed by an in-depth discussion of the quality of the Court's liability assessment.

STRUCTURE AND ORGANIZATION

Sound legal judgments are based on a systematic application of the elements of crimes to a well-documented body of factual findings. Factual findings should be based upon a careful weighing of all of the relevant testimony and other evidence presented at trial. The Judgments of other international criminal tribunals, for example the ICTY, typically follow the format of identification of the specific issue, presentation of the Defense and Prosecution contentions on that point, and detailed analysis justifying a factual finding. That analysis typically involves careful consideration of the credibility of the witnesses offering relevant testimony, and rigorous analysis of documentary evidence, including forensics and other such material, as available.

Falling far below this standard and employing a very different format, the Judgment in Case 002/01 offers a poorly organized, meandering narrative in lieu of clearly structured legal writing. This is disappointing, since one would have expected the five-year process of judicial investigation, trial, deliberation, and Judgment-drafting to produce a more rigorous final product. Unfortunately, even the most generous reader must acknowledge that, as a piece of legal writing, the Case 002/01 Judgment is grossly inadequate.

Much of the Judgment reads strikingly like an ill-documented historical narrative, rather than a structured piece of legal writing based upon well-established best practices in preparation of a final written decision in a complex international criminal proceeding. In a well-reasoned criminal judgment, one expects clearly organized analysis, including a full recitation of the applicable law, systematic consideration of the salient arguments presented by the Parties, a careful weighing of the evidence, a reasoned explanation of why certain evidence was found more credible than other evidence, a thoughtful and transparent application of the law to the facts, and final disposition based upon the analysis. This approach has been established as a generally acknowledged standard of practice in international law, as reflected in the Judgments of virtually all the other internationalized criminal tribunals. This standard has been achieved even in cases where the Court has had to manage a far more voluminous evidentiary record, and assess individual liability in a complex multi-defendant case. Indeed, it is precisely in such massive and complex cases that the greatest degree of organization and rigor in Judgment drafting is required.

Table 8 illustrates the stark difference between the typical organizational approach and the one adopted by the Trial Chamber in Case 002/01, by offering a side-by-side comparison of the principal headers from the Table of Contents in four Judgments from four different tribunals. The organizational problem is not merely a superficial issue of ill-chosen section headers. It permeates every aspect of the narrative construction, as any reader who attempts to digest the 630-page document from start to finish will plainly see. In section after section (even, sometimes, where the header indicates that a legal discussion should follow), the Trial Camber's use of an historical narrative form operates to obscure conflicts in the evidence, disregard critical arguments of the Parties without due considerations, and mask the reasoning relied upon by the Judges to reach their own conclusions. The overall organization of the Judgment appears unclear, disjointed, and at times haphazard, giving the distinct impression that legal staff were assigned to write different parts, but those sections were never successfully forged into a coherent whole.

It is not at all clear, for example, how the various factual, general overview sections scattered throughout the Judgment relate to one another, or why they are placed where they are. Likewise, the placement of legal recitations is baffling. For example, it is not clear why the law of the contextual elements of crimes against humanity is placed within Chapter 4 of the Judgment, entitled "General Overview: 17 April 1975 – 6 January 1979," followed 115 pages later by Chapter 9, entitled "Applicable Law: Crimes Against Humanity," where the Court addresses the underlying offenses. This, in turn, is followed by Chapter 10, entitled "Movement of the Populations (Phase One)," which simply launches into

Table 8. Comparison of Principal Headers from Tables of Contents in the Judgments of Different Internationalized Criminal Tribunal Cases

Martic Judgment (ICTY)[246]	*RUF* Judgment (SCSL)[247]	*Bagosora* Judgment (ICTR)[248]	Case 002/01 Judgment (ECCC)[249]
I. Introduction	I. Introduction	I. Introduction	I. Introduction
II. Applicable Law	II. Context	II. Preliminary Issues	II. Preliminary Issues
III. Factual Findings	III. Applicable Law	III. Factual Findings	III. Historical Background
IV. Responsibility of the Accused	IV. Challenges to the Form of the Indictment	IV. Legal Findings	IV. General Overview: 17 April 1975 – 6 January 1979
V. Sentencing	V. Evaluation of Evidence	V. Verdict	V. Administrative Structures
VI. Disposition	VI. Factual and Legal Findings	VI. Sentencing	VI. Communications Structure
	VII. Responsibility of the Accused		VII. Roles and Functions—Nuon Chea
	VIII. Cumulative Convictions		VIII. Roles and Functions—Khieu Samphan
	IX. Disposition		IX. Applicable Law: Crimes Against Humanity
			X. Movement of the Population (Phase One)
			XI. Movement of the Population (Phase Two)
			XII. Tuol Po Chrey
			XIII. Applicable Law: Individual Criminal Responsibility
			XIV. Joint Criminal Enterprise
			XV. The Criminal Responsibility of Nuon Chea
			XVI. The Criminal Responsibility of Khieu Samphan
			XVII. Cumulative Convictions
			XVIII. Sentencing
			XIX. Civil Party Reparations
			XX. Disposition

"Events of April 17 and Ensuing Days" (10.2), of which the first sub-section is "Implementation" (10.2.1)—not stating implementation of what, though presumably this refers back to the implementation of the policy to evacuate, which was the basis of a finding some hundred pages earlier. Without any contextual or conceptual introduction section, 10.2.1 just launches into a descriptive factual narrative: "On the morning of April 17, 1975 Khmer Rouge forces … attacked and entered Phnom Penh …" There is no indication if this narrative will lead to specific factual findings on evacuation as a whole, or on specific elements charged against the individual Accused, etc. It is as if a legal officer in the Trial Chamber was just assigned to write a narrative account of the attack and then this was pasted into the Judgment.

Above all, what distinguishes the structure of this Judgment from the standard practices of other tribunals is the lack of a coherent structure for organizing the evidence and analysis in a series of factual findings based upon the elements in regard to each charge against the Accused. More specifically, what is also missing is a systematic *weighing* of that evidence based upon clearly articulated legal standards and a discussion of relative credibility. In the almost complete absence of such structured analysis, the basis of the factual findings scattered throughout the Judgment remain largely obscure. Narrative format operates to defeat the juristic analysis, which is the core of a well-reasoned opinion.

A particularly salient illustration of the confusing effect of the form of the narrative can be seen in Chapters 10 through 12 of the Judgment. The first two sub-sections of narrative in Chapter 10 consist of 64 pages of mere summary of the evidence, which the Chamber appears to have found convincing ("appears" because there is no indication that these are specific findings based upon a reasoned analysis of the credibility of the witness testimony cited). The narrative takes the tone of established historical fact, and there is no reference to any other accounts, testimony, discrepancies, or Defense arguments. Witness testimony is simply stated as established, as, for example, in Paragraph 489: "The journey of most evacuees was marked by terror and threats or incidents of violence by Khmer Rouge soldiers. There was evidence of some evacuees walking a certain distance at gunpoint, and of others being beaten by Khmer Rouge. Civil Party Sou Sotheavy attested to the rape of a friend."[250] The footnotes reveal that the Civil Party did not witness the rape she testified to, but rather stated that it had later been reported to her by the victim. Credibility of the account is not considered. Only in Paragraph 520 when the Judgment turns to issues of numbers of victims is there some analysis of the available evidence. Even there, however, the treatment is quite cursory.[251]

Section 10.3 finally addresses the Defense arguments about the purposes of the evacuation at Paragraph 525. Here, there is a substantive analysis of the merits of the Defense contention that the evacuation was justified by military concerns. The Judgment rejects these claims and concludes that the reason for the CPK's evacuation policy was that "its earlier practices and experience of evacuating other areas, and for military, economic and ideological reasons, to allow the leadership better control of the people and to prevent enemies from destabilising CPK forces."[252] This would provide a basis for concluding that the policy of evacuation was criminal because it amounted to an unjustified forcible transfer. The salient question, however, is how the Chamber links the Accused, particularly Khieu Samphan, to a shared intent to accomplish the political goals through criminal means, such as forcible transfer and the other attendant violence that occurred at that time. When these issues are finally addressed in a much later section of the Judgment, devoted to Joint Criminal Enterprise (JCE), the results are hardly satisfactory. The disjointed discussion requires constant referring back and forth to take into account the disparate sections of the Judgment (hundreds of pages apart) that bear upon such fundamental issues as criminal intent.

A major problem throughout the text is that the narrative format used by the Court frequently relies either on passive constructions or attributions to abstract entities (e.g., "the Party" or the "Party Centre" or the "Party leadership") rather than naming the specific individuals involved. While this may be due to the state of the evidence, the Judgment should not conceal this fact by using these sorts of rhetorical devices.

It is two individuals who are on trial, not abstract entities, and it is the obligation of the Court to clearly identify and justify the linkage between institutional decisions and policies and the Accused. As an example of the use of passive constructions, Paragraph 408 concludes that Khieu Samphan was trusted to attend and participate in meetings "where critical decisions were made." The passive construction obscures agency and who actually arrived at the decision or supported it. The Chamber never states that Khieu Samphan played any role in making those decisions, and, in any event, elsewhere in the Judgment it acknowledges that decision-making was not collective and that individuals may have expressed different opinions or dissented (or taken no part though present). The passive construction obscures any attribution of individual agency. The issue is of considerable importance, given that the Defense argues that even if he was at such meetings, he was not playing a participatory role, but inquiry into this salient distinction is covered over by the Judgment's language.

Despite a lengthy preceding narrative and discussion of Khieu Samphan's role, the final conclusion on his role and responsibilities comes as somewhat of an anti-climax that calls into question the legal findings and conclusions arrived at later in the Judgment. At Paragraph 409, the Judgment merely states that despite his high titles, Khieu Samphan's role was largely limited to economy and foreign trade. In regard to his broader authority, all the Chamber can conclude is that, "Through his attendance of Central and Standing Committee meetings, his work in Office 870, his supervision of the Commerce Committee and the content of the speeches he made, he had knowledge of the CPK's policies and access to information about the situation in Cambodia generally, including knowledge of arrests of senior cadres such as KOY Thuon, Doeun and VORN Vet."[253] How does his awareness of policies, awareness that certain individuals were being arrested or disappearing (which would have been fairly widely noticed in Party circles), the admission of the limitation of his role to certain areas, and the recognition that his titles did not reflect *de facto* authority and participation provide the basis for the Judgment's later findings on his participation in the JCE and the crimes charged? The generality of this conclusion obscures more than it explains about the Judgment's chain of reasoning.

Similarly, the discussion in Paragraphs 388-389 purport to demonstrate Khieu Samphan's "awareness" of crimes, implicitly to support an inference of intent or participation. The findings, however, are embedded in a conclusory narrative that, as elsewhere in the Judgment, reads more like an historian's account than a reasoned final decision. There is no clear presentation of the relevant evidence adduced at trial, nor is there any recitation of the arguments raised by either the Prosecution or the Defense on the matter. There is scant analysis of both in order to show the basis of the finding. These are crucial issues and such analysis is sorely lacking. The findings reached here, moreover, and in similar narrative passages in these earlier parts of the Judgment, are later referenced as rock solid conclusions on which legal findings on the elements of the offenses and theories of liability are based.[254]

Another serious issue with the Chamber's narrative approach is that it jumps around in the most bewildering manner, separating parts of the discussion that logically ought to appear in much closer proximity. For example, although the ultimate discussion of the liability of the Khieu Samphan on a JCE theory will come much later, in Chapter 16, the Judgment takes up the issue of what implications the policy behind the evacuation might have for the liability of the Accused in a section entitled "Pre-established Plan and Generalized Policy" (10.3.3). The starting point is the statement that the evacuation of Phnom Penh must be understood as part of the implementation of a policy going back to 1974 to empty all of the towns and cities in Cambodia. The Court's finding on this crucial issue builds upon its previous factual narrative and findings more than 100 pages earlier, and is then connected to the actual legal findings on JCE and Superior Responsibility for the evacuations, situated much later in the Judgment.

One wonders why these lengthy discussions of the evacuation policy are separated according to their dates when the Judgment eventually brings them together here and essentially argues that they must be viewed as part of a whole that predates the Khmer Rouge takeover. Arguing thus that the policy pre-dated April 1975, the Tribunal finds in Paragraph 542 that, "The evacuation of Phnom Penh was no exception insofar as it was carried out pursuant to a predetermined military, economic and ideological strategy whereby all cities that were captured and 'liberated' were subsequently evacuated. Indeed, the decision to evacuate Phnom Penh was developed through meetings starting from June 1974 …"

This finding grounds the rejection of Defense claims as to legitimate reasons for the evacuation of Phnom Penh.[255] The Judgment then immediately moves to a section called "Legal Findings" (10.4). Here, the Court finds that the crimes against humanity of forcible transfer, murder, extermination, persecution, and other inhumane acts occurred during the evacuation of Phnom Penh. Having arrived at this conclusion, the Judgment turns to Phase Two of the movement of populations in Chapter 11, the first section of which returns to a "General Overview" narrative based upon the Regime's policy, as previously articulated in the Judgment. For the most part, it is the personified policy that drives the narrative, and there are scant references to individual roles or to the roles of the Accused in the articulation of the Phase Two policy and its implementation in 1975-1977. This 43-page "General Overview" in the form of a narrative again obscures individual agency rather than highlighting the role of specific individuals or the Accused. It then leads directly to the "Legal Findings" in Section 11.2, which are thus based upon the "General Overview" narrative rather than on focused analysis and weighing of the evidence. The findings on the Accused are deferred to later sections, even though those sections generally do not make independent findings but refer back, in abbreviated form, to the prior narrative.

Repeating this fundamental organizational problem, the section on "Legal Findings" for Phase Two of the evacuations—as in the section on Phase One—takes all the facts in the "General Overview" as established, though they have not been put forward as specific factual findings based upon a reasoned analysis of the evidence, but, rather, as an historical narrative. This bewildering reliance on narrative that assumes facts rather than analyzes evidence to establish them must be seen as a key weakness of the Judgment.

The "Legal Findings" section in Chapter 11 takes only 13 pages to find that all of the crimes against humanity charged did in fact occur, but again there is no attribution of responsibility. These are simply historical events that occurred. Agency is either obscured by passive constructions (e.g., "the Chamber notes that, in many locations, exclusively 'New People' were forcibly transferred" [256]) or attributed to "the CPK leadership "[257] or "Khmer Rouge soldiers and officials"[258] or "the Party."[259] Given the fluidity of the leadership elite and the admittedly obscure and convoluted structures in operation, greater precision is necessary to justify assignment of such sweeping individual criminal liability (especially collating these findings with the very extensive analysis of the Khmer Rouge administrative structures earlier in the Judgment). One would have wished to see a clear picture of precisely how that leadership structure operated in directing Phase Two of the resettlements.

Similar problems emerge in Chapter 12, which turns to the killings at Tuol Po Chrey. In regard to the alleged killings, the Court concludes in a three-page "Legal Findings" section (12.5) that the elements of murder, extermination, and persecution as crimes against humanity have been met. Section 12.5, "Legal Findings," begins by stating that, "The Closing Order charges the Accused with murder, extermination, and political persecution through execution as crimes against humanity …." However, neither of the Accused is ever mentioned in these three pages, which consist of general findings on the basis of the narrative of events at Tuol Po Chrey in sections 12.1-12.4. Those sections do engage in discussion of the credibility of the three witnesses who testified before the Court as to the unfolding of events; however, neither of the Accused is ever mentioned in these sections.

So although the charges against the Accused for Tuol Po Chrey in the Closing Order are referenced, the brief sections on findings do not focus on either Khieu Samphan or Nuon Chea. In other words, no linkage evidence is adduced in these sections to connect either of the Accused in any way to the murders at Tuol Po Chrey. Given that this chapter introduces the "Legal Findings" account by stating that the Accused are charged with the specified crimes, the omission of any mention of them in the "Legal Findings" or narrative of events is striking. It falls then to subsequent sections to provide the basis for connecting the Accused to the movement of populations and the executions at Tuol Po Chrey. Given that the part of the Judgment dealing with pre-1975 events and with the general administrative structures did discuss the Accused in some detail, what is missing here, some 395 pages into the Judgment, is the factual basis and theories of liability that can connect the Accused to the crimes. The two individual Accused have been conspicuously absent from the previous 184 pages of factual findings (i.e., narrative summary in the form of "overviews") and legal findings.

The ensuing section, Chapter 13, "Applicable Law and Individual Responsibility," takes up the theories of liability that will be relied upon to link the Accused to the crimes previously enumerated.[260] However, as discussed in detail below, the quality of the Judgment continues to founder in this section, no doubt in part because it must build upon such a disjointed and unsystematically compiled base of factual findings.

LIABILITY ASSESSMENT

Arguably the most critical aspect of a criminal trial Judgment is the liability assessment, where a trier of fact explains the basis upon which they have reached a conclusion of guilt or acquittal. This can also be the most analytically challenging component, especially when a Tribunal is applying a complex liability theory like Joint Criminal Enterprise to impute constructive liability across a group of alleged perpetrators for a large number of crimes they did not directly order or personally commit. Unfortunately, the liability assessment in the Case 002/01 Judgment is replete with errors, compounded by the fact that the bewildering form of the Judgment narrative makes it difficult to even locate all the necessary components of the legal analysis. As this section of the report will show, scattered throughout the meandering narrative of the Judgment, one finds questionable foundations in law, an extremely weak approach to factual findings, and a totally misguided application of law to facts.

Questionable Foundations in Law

The principal convictions entered against Nuon Chea and Khieu Samphan were based on JCE, a constructive liability theory that received lengthy, but deeply misguided, treatment in the Judgment. Both Accused were also charged under the doctrine of Superior Responsibility. Strangely, despite pages of analysis concluding that Nuon Chea was responsible as a superior for the crimes alleged in the Closing Order, the Judgment does not actually enter a conviction against him on this basis, but relies instead on JCE as the primary theory of responsibility.[261] However, the Judgment does state that it "will consider the Accused's superior position in sentencing." [262]

In international criminal tribunals, there has generally been quite heavy reliance on constructive liability frameworks like these. Some argue that the heavy use of JCE and Superior Responsibility is entirely appropriate because it facilitates convictions of more senior commanders, who are otherwise hard to tie directly to violent acts, and also because these liability frameworks most closely reflect the nature of collective criminality that produces the sort of mass atrocity on trial in international criminal tribunals. Critics, on the other hand, have argued that JCE "is imprecise, dilutes standards of proof, undermines the principle of individual criminal responsibility in favour of collective responsibility, infringes the *nullum crimen sine lege* principle, and infringes the right of the Accused to a fair trial."[263] As some scholars have pointed out, constructive liability theories can "facilitate the conviction of individual villains who have apparently participated in serious violations of human rights. But they result in discounted convictions that inevitably diminish the didactic significance of the Tribunal's Judgments and that compromise its historical legacy."[264] These risks are inherent even when courts *properly* apply complex liability theories, but when they begin with a misconceived notion of an already controversial legal construct, the result is much worse. As the following sections illustrate, the Trial Chamber's flawed conception and application of both JCE and Superior Responsibility in Case 002/01 raised serious concerns about fair trial rights, and most certainly diminished the didactic significance of the Judgment.

Joint Criminal Enterprise

Joint Criminal Enterprise (JCE) was first named and expressly defined at the ICTY, by the *Tadić* Appeals Judgment in 1999.[265] *Tadić* articulated three different forms of JCE—basic (JCE I), systematic (JCE II), and extended (JCE III).[266] Because the crimes alleged at the ECCC predate the *Tadić* case, the ECCC had to consider whether JCE was even a recognized form of liability under customary international law at the time of the alleged crimes. This issue was fiercely contested by the Parties at trial, and is in fact still under contention in the Case 002/01 Appeal. The Trial Chamber's approach to this legal question in the Judgment merits close scrutiny.

JCE and the principle of legality. Both Defense teams argued throughout the trial and in their closing submissions that JCE is not legitimately applied to the cases before the ECCC because it was not a recognized form of criminal liability in the 1970s, and therefore violates the principle of *nullum crimen sine lege*. The Chamber deals briefly with these objections to JCE as a preliminary matter at the beginning of Chapter 13 of the Judgment,[267] noting that this matter had already been considered and ruled upon by the Pre-Trial Chamber (PTC) in May 2010, and subsequently confirmed by the Trial Chamber in September of 2011.[268] The Judgment declines to reconsider the arguments, adopting the same reasoning as the earlier decisions: "Considering the senior positions of the Accused and the customary nature of JCE I and JCE II by 1975, the Chamber finds that this mode of liability was foreseeable and accessible to the Accused."[269] This paragraph in the Judgment gives no indication of what standard it uses to determine whether a legal doctrine was "foreseeable and accessible" to the Accused, but as the 2010 PTC decision on JCE referenced in the footnotes explained:

> In light of its finding that JCE I and II are forms of responsibility that were recognized in customary international law since the post-World War II international instruments and international military case law as discussed above, as well as its earlier finding that these forms of liability have an underpinning in the Cambodian law concept of co-authorship applicable at the time, the Pre-Trial Chamber has no doubt that liability based on

common purpose, design or plan was sufficiently accessible and foreseeable to the defendants.[270]

It is worth questioning why neither the Trial Chamber or the PTC ever surveyed the literature and case law of the 1975-1979 period before reaching the conclusion that JCE was "foreseeable and accessible" to the Accused at that time. Such an examination would have revealed that neither JCE, nor a JCE-like form of liability, appears in the thinking of those discussing war crimes prosecutions in that era. In the 1970s, the American War in Vietnam was a focal point of discussion for liability of military officers and civilian officials. That literature reveals quite clearly that the emphasis was on theories of Command Responsibility. JCE appears neither in name nor in substance. Telford Taylor, who at that time was a law professor at Columbia University, published one of the books that attracted enormous attention in 1970. Because Taylor was not only a formidable scholar but also the former Deputy Prosecutor at Nuremberg and Chief Counsel Prosecutor at the 12 Nuremberg Subsequent Proceedings, his analysis of the responsibility of American commanders and civilian officials for war crimes in Vietnam was taken seriously by the United Stated (US) military establishment.[271] The book generated a considerable law review literature over the next several years concerning the issue of Superior Responsibility in general and the liability of American commanders in particular. Surveying this literature, one will find no reference to such a mode of liability as JCE, as the PTC and Trial Chambers of the ECCC acknowledge in their finding that JCE III was not known in international law in this period.[272]

If one were to take seriously the standard of "foreseeable and accessible," one might imagine that the Indochina wars of 1945-1979, of which the rise of the Khmer Rouge was a part, would have been the obvious reference point for individuals such as the Accused. This would have been only natural because, as is well known, there were repeated allegations of war crimes and crimes against humanity that were made against various nations participating in those wars. As Taylor's book and attendant law review literature indicate, one would search in vain for a reference to JCE in the discussions of such allegations. The Chamber ignores this context in making its finding.

To find that JCE existed in international customary law in 1975 is already a stretch, but it has now been institutionalized in the jurisprudence of the contemporary international and internationalized criminal tribunals for the 1990s, and it is not surprising that the ECCC would extend it back to 1975. But to say that *because* of the senior position of the Accused it was foreseeable and accessible to them begs credulity. In what sense was it "accessible"? The Judgment provides no standard or reasoning on this point beyond saying that the Accused occupied a senior position.

The *Tadić* Appeals Judgment surveyed a number of WWII war crimes trials, and brought what it saw as three different theories of liability under one nomenclature as JCE I, JCE II, and JCE III. Considerable barriers to the prior "accessibility" of the concept of JCE are readily apparent on the face of the *Tadić* Appeals Judgment, which recounts how Judge Cassese in fact had to send researchers physically to visit the British National Archives and other such repositories to unearth the records of obscure cases from British and Italian post-WWII trials.[273] These records had never previously been published, and in the case of the British records on which the *Tadić* Appeals Judgment most heavily relies, had not even been declassified until 1974.[274] Is the standard of accessibility that Khieu Samphan and Nuon Chea could in theory have traveled to the British Public Records Office and spent months sifting through the WWII cases to anticipate the reasoning that Cassese would later use in the *Tadić* Appeals Judgment? This is literally what would have been required to "foresee" the application of JCE as a theory of liability.

The brute fact is that the only readily accessible and relevant records in 1975 would have been the Judgments of the International Military Tribunal at Nuremberg (IMT) and the International Military Tribunal for the Far East (IMTFE) in Tokyo (the latter of which would have required access to a major research library or knowledge of Japanese). The records of the Nuremberg Subsequent Proceedings were also accessible in a number of repository libraries at major US universities after the printing of a limited edition by the US Government Printing Office in 1951. Yet these foundational documents for the only international criminal proceedings held before 1993 make no reference to JCE, because the indictments charged conspiracy, not JCE, as the theory of liability aimed at the leadership echelons of Japan and Germany. It is telling that the *Tadić* Appeals Judgment does not discuss these cases and their reliance on conspiracy theory, but turns instead to a small number of obscure trials held before British, American, and, secondarily, Italian military courts. What makes that exercise methodologically questionable (to put it mildly) is that these British and American military commissions produced no Judgments or final written decisions explaining the basis of their verdicts. Accordingly, these courts never state what theory of liability they relied upon. Since no one before Cassese had brought these cases together under one conceptual umbrella and categorized them according to three forms of an overarching theory of liability, it is difficult to imagine on what rational basis the Chamber finds that they were "accessible and foreseeable" to the Accused because of their "senior positions."

Nonetheless, having decided that JCE I is applicable to the cases at the ECCC, and does not violate the principle of legality in the opinion of the Trial Chamber, the Judgment continues with its application of the doctrine throughout Chapters 13, 14, 15, and 16. Unfortunately, the Chamber's application of this already controversial liability theory reveals serious analytical shortcomings, stemming mostly from the Chamber's ill-conceived approach to defining the common criminal purpose of the alleged JCE.

Common criminal purpose. As the Trial Chamber correctly recites in Paragraph 692 of the Judgment, the basic form of JCE liability requires a finding that a plurality of persons shared a common purpose, "which amounts to or involves the commission of a crime." Moreover, "an accused must have participated in the common purpose, making a significant, but not necessarily indispensable, contribution." At Paragraph 694, the Judgment further notes, "With respect to the *mens rea* for JCE I, an accused must intend to participate in the common purpose and this intent must be shared with the other JCE participants." Prior international case law has established and affirmed that a common plan to commit crimes under a JCE need not be found to have been articulated in advance via an explicit agreement. A commonly held criminal purpose may arise extemporaneously,[275] and may be subsequently inferred from the facts about the behavior of the members of the JCE plurality.[276] However, none of this negates the obligation that falls to the Trial Chamber to specifically examine whether or not each of the Accused knew about the criminal plans, *shared the intent* to commit those crimes, and with that intent made a substantial contribution to the common plan in furtherance of that criminal intent.[277] In Case 002/01, the ECCC totally neglected to complete these vital steps in the liability analysis for the specific Accused, Nuon Chea and Khieu Samphan.

Chapter 14 is entitled "Joint Criminal Enterprise." This is the primary location where the Chamber sets out the nature and scope of the alleged JCE. The beginning of the chapter describes the JCE in the broadest possible terms: "According to the Closing Order, the common purpose of the CPK during the DK era (17 April 1975 to 6 January 1979) was to implement rapid socialist revolution through a 'great leap forward' and defend the Party against internal and external enemies, by whatever means necessary."[278]

This purpose, which is obviously not criminal, is followed by a paragraph describing two policies that the JCE participants allegedly designed and implemented:

> As limited in Case 002/01, the Closing Order alleges that JCE participants designed and implemented the following policies, among others, during the DK era: i. The repeated movement of the population from towns and cities to rural areas, as well as from one rural area to another ("Population Movement Policy"), insofar as this policy is relevant to movement of population (phase one) and movement of population (phase two) (Section 14.2); and ii. The targeting of former officials of the Khmer Republic, including both civil servants and former military personnel and their families ("Targeting Policy"), insofar as this policy is relevant to executions of former Khmer Republic officials at Tuol Po Chrey (Section 14.3).[279]

The first part on movement of populations is also not inherently criminal because the language used does not preclude that there was a legitimate purpose for the movements. The second policy implicates forcible transfers and executions, but even here, the language is imprecise, stating only that the policy "is relevant to" the crimes. The paragraph says that JCE participants designed and implemented the policies, but it does not state that they did so as part of the common purpose that defined the JCE or that the common purpose encompassed the implementation of the criminal policies. This is of course the crucial test for the application of JCE. Given the articulation of a non-criminal common purpose for the JCE, the Chamber must link that purpose to criminal activity *encompassed within the shared intent* of the members of the JCE, including the Accused.

This following section (14.1) begins by restating the common purpose in slightly different terms than two paragraphs earlier:

> The Party leadership pursued a common purpose to liberate Cambodia and create a socialist society in four phases: party-building (September 1960 – January 1968) (Section 14.1.1), initiation of the armed revolution (January 1968 – March 1970) (Section 14.1.2), the democratic revolution (March 1970 – April 1975) (Section 14.1.3) and the socialist revolution (April 1975 – January 1979) (Section 14.1.4).[280]

The Judgment then explains that the ECCC has jurisdiction only over the fourth phase: socialist revolution. The severance that created Case 002/01 further temporally limited this scope of inquiry to between 17 April 1975 and December 1977. However, the Trial Chamber says that in order to understand the JCE it is necessary to trace the earlier phases of evolution since "the most significant participants" joined before April 1975.[281]

The Chamber then embarks on a lengthy discussion, tracing each of the four phases in great detail, going back to 1958. One can only wonder why this historical account is disconnected from the extensive prior history of the Khmer Rouge and biographies of the Accused and the detailed account of their roles and of the evolution of the Khmer Rouge administrative regime, some 200 pages earlier in the Judgment. The first three phases largely cover much of the same ground detailed before and indicate the way in which the Khmer Rouge leadership evolved its idea of revolution. Relevance to the charges against the Accused seems tenuous and the overlap and disjuncture from the previous historical overview again indicates the lack of coherent organization and precision in the Judgment.

Only in Paragraph 736 does the Judgment actually begin the analysis of the JCE in the time period under the jurisdiction of the Court. Paragraph 737 details the main features of the policies informing this new phase of "socialist revolution," but these features are credited abstractly to "the CPK leaders," "the Khmer Rouge leaders," and "the CPK leadership," and even here, *not one* of the policies mentioned is criminal. Instead, the Judgment declares that in the period 1975-1977 the Khmer Rouge leaders, including Khieu Samphan and Nuon Chea, "in speeches, interviews and statements, publicly confirmed and endorsed the party line to rapidly build and defend the country through a socialist revolution based on the principles of secrecy, independence-sovereignty, self-reliance and collectivization."[282] In other words, the Trial Chamber found that the two Accused made public statements affirming and endorsing a non-criminal political program.

In Section 14.2.4 the Chamber again indicates that it will make legal findings as to the JCE. Paragraph 804 repeats the "legal findings" of Paragraph 777 that there was a JCE, and then adds:

> [I]t has also been established that while this common purpose was not criminal in itself, the policies formulated by the Khmer Rouge involved the commission of a crime as a means of bringing the common plan to fruition. These policies resulted in and/or involved the commission of crimes, including forced transfers, murders, attacks against human dignity and political persecution. Both population movements (phases one and two) followed a consistent pattern of conduct in each case including and involving the commission of crimes. This confirms that these policies were criminal and had been adopted beforehand in order to ensure that the common purpose would be achieved.[283]

What has been missing in the analysis up to this point is a finding that individual members of the JCE (in particular the Accused), shared the *intent* to use the criminal means alleged to carry out the common purpose of revolution. While it may have been shown that crimes occurred as a result of the policies, it has not been adequately established that the 18 named members of the JCE all commonly intended these crimes to be the means for the implementation of the policies. In Paragraph 805, the Judgment attempts to make this link in regard to murder. The Chamber states that the population transfers were "pursuant to the Party leadership's" instructions and policy, and that murders resulted from the inhuman conditions of the transfers. On this basis they state, "*Party policy* intended that such suffering and sacrifice would re-educate the 'New People' and attack the class system."[284] (emphasis added) On what basis has it been established that the policy of suffering and sacrifice (which again is not inherently criminal) proves that those implementing the policies intended for murders to occur? A "Party policy" cannot intend anything. A "Party policy" is not on trial. Individuals have intent, criminal or otherwise, which they implement through policies and other actions. The intent of the individuals is what must be proven for a criminal conviction to be entered. The policy may have "resulted" in murders, but that alone is insufficient to establish that such crimes were in fact intended as a common purpose by all of the members of the alleged JCE plurality, which allegedly included the Accused.

The plans and policies are thus never adequately defined in the Judgment as criminal. The most simple and sound formulation would have been to define the common purpose as something *inherently* criminal, but the ECCC chose to emulate a much more convoluted approach taken by the Special Court for Sierra Leone (SCSL), which in the case of *Prosecutor v. Sesay, Kallon, and Gbao*, led to some serious violations of the culpability principle and thus the fair trial rights of the Accused.[285] If some of the CPK leadership aimed to bring about a socialist revolution but did not in fact intend the specific criminal means described in the Closing Order to achieve this goal, then, by definition, they could not be considered members of the JCE plurality, and they should therefore fall outside the scope of constructive liability defined by the JCE.

It is incumbent upon the Chamber to establish beyond a reasonable doubt that all of the crimes alleged in the indictment, crimes going well beyond the evacuations themselves, were commonly intended and therefore encompassed in the common purpose of the JCE. (We may note in passing that the Chamber rarely refers to the standard of proof beyond a reasonable doubt or states specifically why it has been met.) This is because the Chamber confines itself, as it must, to the "basic" form of JCE (JCE I). If the charges against the Accused could be based upon a theory of JCE III then it would have been possible to show that although crimes against humanity committed in the course of the evacuations (apart from the forcible evacuations themselves) were *not* intended within the common purpose, they were nonetheless foreseeable to specific members of the JCE. For JCE I, however, all of the crimes alleged must be encompassed within the common purpose, shared by all the members of the JCE, either directly or as the intended means by which the common purpose was to be fulfilled. As we will discuss further below, particularly in regard to Khieu Samphan, but also in regard to Nuon Chea for certain crimes, the Chamber has difficulty in applying this standard and wanders off into the "forbidden territory" of JCE III-like argumentation.

Superior Responsibility

As with JCE, the Trial Chamber's discussion of the law of Superior Responsibility is predicated on dubious legal foundations, and leaves much to be desired in terms of intellectual rigor. In Pre-Trial motions and again at the close of Trial, the Nuon Chea Defense challenged the applicability of Superior Responsibility on the grounds that this mode of liability was not sufficiently clearly defined in customary international law at the time of the Khmer Rouge. The Defense supported its argument, in part, with reference to divergent standards for *mens rea* espoused in two separate Superior Responsibility cases that pre-dated 1975—the *Medina* Case,[286] arising out of the prosecutions for the My Lai Massacre, and the *Yamashita* Case from World War II.[287] In the Case 002/01 Judgment, the Court summarily dismisses the Defense objection in paragraphs 718-719, but the reasoning of the Chamber is rather anemic, and strongly suggests that the Chamber has conducted no serious research into the relevant jurisprudence on this matter. First of all, they cite not the actual case record of the *Medina* trial, but rather the case "as reported" in Friedman's 1972 compendium on the Law of War. They also cite the US Supreme Court decision in the *Yamashita* Case without noting that the cited decision was merely a rejection of the *habeas corpus* petition. The Case 002/01 Judgment does not cite the decision of the Military Court that convicted Yamashita, which is of course the relevant document for establishing which *mens rea* standard was applied in the conviction.

The conviction of General Yamashita for war crimes committed by Japanese forces in the Philippines from October 1944 to the end of the Second World War (WWII) does, in fact, manifest a lack of clarity as to the appropriate *mens rea* standard, articulating in different parts of that short decision different apparent standards to justify the verdict of guilt. The *Yamashita* Case was the subject of intense discussion in the 1970s as part of a debate in the legal literature of that period of the Vietnam War era on what in fact was the correct *mens rea* standard. This literature arose largely because Telford Taylor had argued that Yamashita was convicted on the basis of a strict liability standard, and that standard should in turn be applied against American commanders in Vietnam.[288] This argument, coming from a former Brigadier General who had served as Deputy Chief Prosecutor at the IMT and Chief Prosecutor for the US in the Nuremberg Subsequent Proceedings, understandably provoked some consternation in American military circles, coming, as it did, in the aftermath of the My Lai Massacre and the attendant trials and cover-up. Military lawyers responded to Taylor with a spate of law review articles reviewing some of the extensive WWII jurisprudence and arguing that the correct *mens rea* standard was either "knowledge" or "negligence," not strict liability. This literature was contemporaneous with the Khmer Rouge period. And it clearly indicates that there was in fact no clarity in the existing international case law as to the definition of *mens rea* for Command Responsibility, as it was then known.

If the Chamber had conducted a review of the WWII jurisprudence that was the only existing relevant case law for 1975-1979, such a review would have easily revealed the merits of Nuon Chea's argument through simply comparing some of the leading cases. The most important, well-known, and easily accessible cases treating this issue in depth are the *High Command* Case[289] and the *Hostage* Case[290] in the Nuremberg Subsequent Proceedings. Their holdings on this issue go directly contrary to the *Yamashita* Case and to other major WWII Command Responsibility trials such as the *Homma* Case,[291] the U.S. trials of Toyoda and Tamura at Tokyo,[292] and the British and Australian trials of Japanese generals.[293]

There would have been, however, no need for the ECCC to actually review such cases directly because the ICTY Trial and Appeals Chambers had already exhaustively treated this issue. The ICTY *Celebici* Appeals Judgment established itself as the leading case on Superior Responsibility a decade and a half ago.[294] There, the Appeals Chamber reviewed the very extensive discussion of the WWII case law and other authorities on the *mens rea* for Superior Responsibility, which had been conducted by the Trial Chamber.[295] The Appeals Chamber disagreed with the assessment of the Trial Chamber on the *mens rea* requirement, and found that the chaotic nature of the WWII jurisprudence on the subject precluded deriving a clear standard from the case law of that era.

As already noted above, rather than resolve the competing *mens rea* standards, the Vietnam era only exacerbated and highlighted the problem. It seems quite clear that the Defense submissions on the status of the law in 1975 had considerable merit, and it is surprising that the Chamber ignored an extremely well-known ICTY Appeals Chamber Judgment, which is widely recognized to be the leading case on this subject. Instead, adopting the reasoning of the ECCC Pre-Trial Chamber from a previous decision, the Trial Chamber concluded that the cases cited were not sufficient to indicate a lack of clarity in the norm, and therefore the Defense argument was dismissed as being without merit.[296] This decision reveals both a lack of rigorous research and a lack of knowledge as to the basic case bearing upon the status of Command Responsibility in the 1975-1979 period.

Weak Foundation for Factual Findings

Moving on from the issue of questionable legal foundations in the Judgment, an equally troubling aspect of the liability assessment is the base of factual findings upon which the conviction relies. Much of the Judgment reads as a document produced by fact-finders not deeply or systematically engaged with the evidentiary record at all. A strong foundation of factual findings is of course essential to the liability assessment, because the Court must be able to link facts systematically to the legal elements of the crimes charged, so as to justify conviction or acquittal (whichever outcome the weight of the facts demands). The whole point of a trial, with all its exacting rules of procedure, is to create a reliable process for collecting and weighing evidence that can be used to prove (or not prove) pertinent facts beyond a reasonable doubt. This is a threshold of proof that should command a great deal of respect for the factual findings and corresponding legal conclusions. It is therefore deeply troubling when the Judgment produced by a lengthy and expensive trial process offers such a weak foundation for its factual findings. A close reading of the

Judgment reveals a number of troubling issues with the evidentiary analysis, including (1) repeated failures to resolve conflicting or internally inconsistent accounts, and (2) a strong tendency toward vagueness and lack of precision, including a failure to justify the findings by reference to specific weighing of the evidence; and failure to specify how the burden of proof beyond a reasonable doubt was met in regard to what other inferences, if any, could plausibly be drawn from the evidence on which the Court chose to rely.

Conflicting accounts and internal inconsistencies

Failure to reconcile conflicting evidence, or address internally inconsistent testimony, is a problem that runs through the entire Judgment. One encounters poor or missing analysis of these conflicts, and sorely inadequate explanations for why the Trial Chamber weighed the evidence as it did. For example, the Trial Chamber struggles throughout the Judgment to pinpoint the precise functions and personnel of the Khmer Rouge leadership, including almost complete confusion and contradiction between expert witnesses as to the nature of the so-called "Office 870."[297] The Chamber follows the opinion of expert David Chandler who testified that the code name "Office 870" was part of the policy of secrecy and was used to "conceal or obscure the true nature of the CPK leadership." This concealment was obviously effective as the Court is unable to determine what Office 870 meant. While Chandler and another expert, Philip Short, describe Office 870 as a "nerve center" and say it had a "critically important role" in transmitting information to the Standing Committee, there is a great deal of confusion as to whether it was the same or distinct from "Committee 870," "Bureau 870," "M 870," and other Khmer Rouge bodies. The underlying problem here is, as the Chamber recognizes, the CPK leadership's obsession with secrecy and concealing true lines of authority and the actual role of specific individuals. While it is one thing for historians like Chandler, Short, and Stephen Heder[298] to develop interpretations that aim at unraveling the bureaucratic maze of obfuscation embodied in the various designations of individuals and entities, it is another thing for a court to claim factual findings to a legal standard beyond a reasonable doubt. The difficulty experienced by these experts, who have spent decades analyzing the Khmer Rouge and the structures of authority through which they operated, illustrates the challenge faced by the Chamber.

The struggle to confront contradictions and internal inconsistencies is also apparent in other passages where the Chamber acknowledges the difficulty in penetrating the shroud of "Angkar." Although this term is well known, the Chamber recognizes that it functioned as a shroud of secrecy to conceal who was actually responsible for the policies and actions attributed to the anonymous "Angkar." Although virtually every account of the history of the Khmer Rouge refers to "Angkar" as a designation widely used to identify the source of policies and decisions, there is nonetheless still so much confusion as to exactly what that term meant and how it was used.[299] The Chamber notes the confused and contradictory testimony of witnesses, which it attributes to this policy of secrecy, but the Judgment does not squarely address the evidentiary implications of the widely shared confusion. How can the Chamber manage to support findings beyond a reasonable doubt as to the liability of specific individuals when a myriad of bureaucratic designations were deliberately used by the Khmer Rouge precisely to obfuscate the roles of these same persons?

The Chamber acknowledges the factual opaqueness in its limited conclusions about the key role of Standing Committee members in the DK era:

In light of the evidence given by NUON Chea, KHIEU Samphan and IENG Sary – all of whom attended or participated in meetings of the Standing Committee – the Chamber is satisfied that key decisions of the Standing Committee were not simply made unilaterally by POL Pot, but rather were made collectively; that is to say, with the input of, and with a broad consensus from, the entire Committee. *However, the Chamber is unable to conclude that unanimity was required in decision-making, and therefore leaves open the possibility that individual members may have disagreed with particular decisions from time to time.* (emphasis added)[300]

This is a noteworthy qualification because elsewhere in the Judgment, in its account of the evacuation of Phnom Penh, the Court refers to collective decision-making as the principle by which it is able to include Khieu Samphan as "participating" in the decision, absent any concrete evidence of what he actually said or did.[301] Indeed, analysis of credible evidence as to the nature, if any, of Khieu Samphan's substantive "participation" at any of the meetings he attended is entirely lacking. Equally lacking is a reasoned analysis of what other inferences can be drawn from his physical presence at meetings other than the inference drawn by the Judgment. The discussion and weighing of such inferences is a standard part of justifying factual findings in typical tribunal practice, and is necessary to explain why there is no reasonable doubt as to the specific finding made by the Court.

Evidence for the decision to evacuate the cities is discussed at Paragraphs 135-147, and these passages make clear how tenuous the basis of the Chamber's legal conclusion on JCE really is. To begin with, the evidence as to whether Khieu Samphan was even at the key June 1974 meeting is conflicting, leaving aside the complete absence of evidence cited as to the nature of his participation. This problem is exacerbated by the fact that the Judgment does not detail and weigh the conflicting Defense evidence, nor does it make specific findings on why that evidence is not credible. The Judgment only notes the conflicting testimony as to whether he was even there. It does not consider the case made by the Defense and weigh the case against the evidence it has chosen to rely on.

In Paragraph 135 the Chamber states that, "There were conflicting accounts as to whether KHIEU Samphan attended the meeting at which the decision to evacuate Phnom Penh was made."[302] Khieu Samphan testified that he was out of the country when the meeting took place. The testimony of Nuon Chea supported this contention, and Nuon Chea further stated that Khieu Samphan did not know of the decision made in regard to evacuation. Contradicting these pieces of evidence, the Chamber notes that witness Phy Phuon testified that Khieu was at the meeting and supported the decision. The Chamber accepts the evidence that Khieu was repeatedly traveling outside of the country in April-June 1974, and it finds that he was in fact in Lao People's Democratic Republic the first week of June, but it then states that it finds it "likely" that the meeting was scheduled so that Khieu could be there.[303]

Why was it "likely"? Apart from the fact that the exact date of the meeting in June is not even known, the Chamber has no concrete evidence to support this finding, nor is there any explanation as to why a finding of "likelihood" would meet the burden of proof beyond a reasonable doubt on this crucial fact. Also dismissing the evidence of Khieu Samphan's wife that he in fact first returned to Cambodia in July 1974, the Chamber concludes that he was present at the June 1974 meeting and participated in the decision to evacuate the cities. The only evidence relied on by the Chamber as to Khieu Samphan's involvement in the alleged decision is that according to the "principle of democratic centralism" he "acceded." This unsubstantiated theory of monolithic decision-making runs throughout the Judgment and provides the means for attributing decisions to the Accused in instances where there is no evidence as to their actual participation. As seen above, in a later part of the Judgment, the Court contradicts itself and finds that it cannot conclude that there was such an operative principle.

In other words, in regard to the specific meeting in June 1974, the Chamber references absolutely no evidence as to what, if Khieu Samphan was in fact present, either he or Nuon Chea actually said or how the decision was taken. The Chamber's finding that the decision to evacuate was made at the June 1974 meeting appears to be contradicted by the next section of the Judgment, which turns to another meeting in February 1975. Here the Chamber states that the evacuation of the cities was again discussed by the "CPK in February 1975. Although Expert David CHANDLER recognized that opinions differ about this date, it was his view that the decision to evacuate the cities was made in February 1975."[304] This, of course, conflicts with what the Chamber has just concluded in regard to the decision having been made in June 1974 with Khieu Samphan's participation. No explanation is given and the conflict in the testimony is not discussed. Instead, the Chamber immediately turns to the meeting in "early April 1975."

The Chamber concludes that it was at the April 1975 meeting that the plan to evacuate Phnom Penh was approved. In regard to Khieu Samphan's presence, which the Defense denied, the Chamber relies only on the testimony of witness Phy Phuon, who himself did not attend the meeting because of his low-ranking position. Based on a finding that Phy Phoun was in the "vicinity," the Chamber accepts Phy Phoun's suggestion that he could observe and hear what was said from his position outside the meeting place. He testified that Khieu Samphan supported the plan and, along with the other participants, applauded to indicate his assent.

Given that the testimony of this witness is the *only* evidence contradicting the testimony that Khieu Samphan was not even at the meeting, one would expect a careful weighing of the credibility of this witness and an equally careful weighing of that evidence as against the credibility of the other testimony. Instead, there are only a few lines in a footnote devoted to this important issue, and the Defense arguments contesting this point are only briefly alluded to in passing.[305] In those lines, the Chamber states that it found that Phy's testimony in Court was "largely consistent" with the testimony he gave to the investigating Judge. What, exactly, does "largely consistent" mean and what is the standard the Chamber is using to weigh his credibility? One will find no answer to these questions in the Judgment. One will also find no detailed discussion of where Phy was positioned, how he got there, what he could see or hear from that vantage point, or how long he was there. These are the kinds of considerations that one would expect the Judgment to focus on, in relation, of course, to the required standard of proof beyond a reasonable doubt. The Chamber, on the other hand, only notes his testimony that the meeting took place in an "ordinary shed" and that he was "consistent in his statements that he was able to see and hear everything inside."[306]

Phy may have been "consistent," but the relevant legal question the Trial Chamber ought to have been asking is whether his account is *credible*. Here the Chamber does not engage in a specific analysis about the nature of the meeting place, the placement of the witness in regard to his ability to see and hear, why he would have been allowed to see and hear this meeting, and other similar issues. The point is that, despite declarations made throughout the trial that the Chamber would undertake a careful weighing of probative value of all evidence used to form the basis of convictions against the Accused, here is a concrete and consequential example where the Chamber fails to conduct such analysis. There is no standard articulated as to how credibility is being weighed, no discussion of whether and why the evidence meets the burden of proof, and the Defense's arguments are not taken into account and weighed against the other evidence.

In regard to the key issue of participation of the Accused in policy formulation and decision-making related to the JCE and the crimes charged, there is a sharp contradiction in the Court's findings. On the one hand, we find the Court's broad liability extrapolations in the evacuation discussion, based on its finding that the CPK made unanimous collective decisions on the basis of "democratic centralism." On the other hand, the Chamber makes qualified findings about the Standing Committee later in the Judgment, at Paragraph 228, holding that "the Chamber is unable to conclude that unanimity was required in decision-making, and therefore leaves open the possibility that individual members may have disagreed with particular decisions from time to time." [307]

The depth of factual uncertainty that remains about crucial aspects of the Khmer Rouge leadership structures and how they functioned is particularly troubling in light of the fact that the Court bases its JCE liability on mere participation in meetings where policies were decided, yet the Court has no particular insight into how or by whom those decisions were taken. The Khieu Samphan Defense, in particular, pointedly and consistently contested allegations about his actual position and authority. The Judgment gives ample reason to doubt even inferences of mere acquiescence, let alone shared intent, from Khieu Samphan's attendance at meetings.[308] Since the Chamber is unable to adduce evidence as to what Khieu Samphan said at such meetings, the possibility that he could have, in fact, had or voiced a different opinion from the policy decided upon is crucial for his liability in general and for his alleged membership in the JCE in particular.[309] The Chamber nowhere considers what other plausible inferences could be drawn from the evidence at hand, nor does it engage in a general discussion of its standards regarding inferences.

One also must question the Trial Chamber's unexplained, selective disregard for a single exculpatory aspect of testimony from an expert witness whose opinion the Trial Chamber otherwise generally accepted and relied upon. Along with David Chandler, Philip Short was one of two main expert witnesses on whom the Chamber chose to rely heavily in its Judgment. Nevertheless, at Paragraph 152, the Trial Chamber declares that:

> While Philip SHORT considered that KHIEU Sampan was not part of the decision-making apparatus, the Chamber does not find KHIEU Samphan's statements that he was entirely ignorant of the plans to evacuate Phnom Penh credible. Given his close relationship with NUON Chea, POL Pot, and IENG Sary, and the evidence summarized above, the Chamber is satisfied that NUON Chea, as well as Khieu Sampan and IENG Sary, participated in the decision to evacuate Phnom Penh and other urban centres.[310]

This paragraph contains a key finding that the Chamber relies heavily upon in its JCE liability assessment against the two Accused. Although the Chamber accepts and adopts the majority of Short's opinions elsewhere in the Judgment, here, where the expert witness had expressed an exculpatory opinion about the Accused, Khieu Samphan, the Chamber suddenly rejects Short's opinion without giving any explanation for why it found this particular aspect of his testimony unpersuasive or lacking in credibility. Of course, if the Court had adopted the expert witness opinion on this point, it would have undermined the whole theory of JCE liability used to convict Khieu Samphan, by casting reasonable doubt on his role in the series of events leading up to the mass population movements adjudicated in Case 002/01. The only apparent reason for rejecting this piece of Short's expert testimony is that it conflicted with the Chamber's own preferred conclusion about the liability of the Accused. This is hardly the kind of well-reasoned finding one would expect on an issue so crucial to determining the liability of an accused person.

Vagueness and lack of precision throughout highly consequential sections of factual findings
Another major flaw of the Judgment is its failure to articulate precise factual findings on highly consequential matters, fundamental to the ultimate assignment of liability. These include: (1) precise structures of authority and specific roles of the Accused in DK; (2) participation and intent of the Accused in decisions about population movements; (3) knowledge and intent with respect to killings at Tuol Po Chrey.

Precise structures of authority and specific roles. As noted above, the Chamber's discussion of the Military Committee and other bodies left considerable confusion as to the membership and functions of some apparently important Khmer Rouge institutions or administrative entities. What this means is that, although one can make an organogram of the DK "structures," the trial produced very little insight or clarity about how the various roles were populated, and how the organization operated. These facts are vitally important, in particular for Superior Responsibility, because liability should not be based upon formal position, mere membership, or nominal titles, but rather upon *de facto* command authority and the way that it was exercised and recognized in specific situations. For Khieu Samphan's liability, the issues arises nowhere more acutely than in regard to his relation to the Standing Committee. This issue is crucial both because of the key function of the Standing Committee and because it was so heavily contested by the Prosecution and Defense. What is at stake here is whether Khieu Samphan actually did affirmatively participate in the key policy and other decisions that could establish a common purpose, which resulted in the commission of crimes. Without such a finding the entire case against him based upon JCE evaporates.

The way the Court deals with this issue, however, does justice neither to the Defense case, which is not fully considered point-by-point in relation to the Prosecution case, nor to what one would expect in terms of a well-reasoned argument. While the Judgment ultimately makes a finding that is the basis for inculpating Khieu Samphan, it is never clear what standard the Chamber is using to weigh the specific evidence. It does not consider, as noted above, whether the interpretation it adopts is the only plausible inference that can be drawn from the evidence.[311] Instead, it just accepts one set of inferences as advanced by the Prosecution without weighing it against other inferences that could be drawn from the available evidence, as required by the burden of proof beyond a reasonable doubt.

While the Judgment acknowledges that "KHIEU Samphan was never formally a member of the CPK Standing Committee,"[312] it goes on to state that, "He has admitted that he attended what he described as 'open' or 'expanded' meetings of the Standing Committee, but has consistently asserted that he did not voice opinions or participate in decision-making during those meetings."[313] What is the evidence, then, that contradicts his testimony and establishes that he actually meaningfully or fully participated in the decision- and policy-making of the Standing Committee? The Judgment states that, "The Co-Prosecutors allege that KHIEU Samphan was a *de facto* member of the Standing Committee and that his attendance of its meetings placed him within a small group of powerful and fully-informed members of the Party Centre."

In support of this proposition, the Chamber notes that Khieu Samphan was present at many of the documented Standing Committee meetings during the period for which there are minutes (August 1975 to June 1976).[314] Apart from the fact that mere presence does not undermine the Defense position, a major problem left unresolved by the Judgment is that these minutes do not cover all of the meetings in that period, and some of them do not list those who attended. Moreover, the minutes only cover this 10-month period. The Court, however, specifically infers from this 10-month period that he continued to regularly attend thereafter. What is the basis for this inference? Based on the evidence and arguments of the Defense and Prosecution, are there other plausible inferences? The Judgment is largely silent on this point. Given the volatility over time within the CPK's leadership echelons, as amply demonstrated by the Judgment's own findings, what concrete evidence supports such an important inference? The Court again fails to base its finding on a reasoned argument that weighs all the evidence, pro and con. It also fails, again, to articulate or apply a clear standard on which it bases its findings establishing facts beyond a reasonable doubt.

What the Court does instead is argue that, "The surviving minutes demonstrate that, despite his insistence to the contrary, KHIEU Samphan actively participated in some Standing Committee meetings. Although the minutes do not always attribute remarks to individual speakers, they prove that KHIEU Samphan contributed on *at least two occasions*, reporting to the Committee on relations with NORODOM Sihanouk and on the 'election' of 20 March 1976."[315] (emphasis added) This evidence, based on *two* remarks in 23 meetings, hardly supports the Chamber's conclusions, let alone demonstrating that he actually participated in decisions. Indeed, both instances show him merely reporting on political events to the Standing Committee. This is consistent with the political role he described himself as filling and the reason, on his account, that he was asked to attend Standing Committee meetings.

What other inferences might one have plausibly drawn? From the fact that he may have only spoken twice in 23 meetings, one could also plausibly infer that he, as a non-member, attended some Standing Committee meetings when asked to do so, consistent with the political role he occupied. One could also plausibly infer that such minor participation indicates that he did not share authority, influence, or decision-making capacity with the inner circle of the CPK leadership. This is, of course, precisely what he testified to, and what the Defense argued at trial. Does the paltry evidence introduced by the Chamber and the inferences drawn from it credibly support their conclusion of his crucial role at the heart of the CPK leadership? The Chamber adduces no evidence that he participated in decision-making at these meetings, nor does it systematically weigh the competing testimony and arguments or justify the inferences it makes.

Vagueness and lack of precision continue to be a problem in the Judgment when the Court turns to the issue of control in regard to the evacuation of Phnom Penh. During that period, the Judgment finds, Phnom Penh was under military control of Zone secretaries who "sought and received instructions" from Pol Pot, Nuon Chea, and other senior leaders. Khieu Samphan is not mentioned.[316] The Judgment further finds that Pol Pot, Nuon Chea, Ieng Sary, and Khieu Samphan at this time formed a "Joint Leadership Committee. On a regular basis, along with various Zone and Autonomous Sector secretaries and others, they met to discuss policies and plans to build and defend a self-reliant, independent and socialist country, such as the establishment of cooperatives."[317] This does little more than say that they worked together to implement the policies of the socialist revolution. The relevance to the crimes allegedly linked to the JCE is not made clear.

Paragraph 743 provides the first, tenuous link of Khieu Samphan to the evacuations when it finds that he and many other leaders attended a large meeting at the Silver Pagoda, where "reasons justifying the evacuations of the cities were provided." This does little to indicate intent on his part or any affirmative participation whatsoever in the decision or policy about evacuation. As the language of the Judgment indicates, justifications were provided for a decision. This was not a decision-making meeting. No argument or evidence is provided as to how this attendance proves his intention in regard to the commission of crimes allegedly encompassed in the JCE. Footnotes 2341 and 2342 both cite witnesses who indicate that Pol Pot and Nuon Chea were the ones who lectured and who led these meetings. These witnesses do not mention Khieu Samphan at all.

In Paragraph 745, the Chamber attempts to buttress its findings in regard to Khieu Samphan, holding that beginning around August 1975, the Standing Committee began to meet and Khieu Samphan attended these meetings "on a regular basis." Notwithstanding the fact that previous sections of the Judgment focusing on these meetings indicated problems related to Khieu Samphan's attendance, in this section his attendance is now labeled as "regular." This finding in regard to Khieu Samphan illustrates the Court's failure to contend squarely and transparently with mixed evidence. There is no analysis of the evidence here to justify this key finding that will undergird the Judgment's later conclusion as to his liability predicated upon attendance.

The separation of several hundred pages of these related sections making such findings operates to obscure the facts, which reveal a very strained interpretation in regard to the inferences that could be drawn from Khieu Samphan's attendance. One could also characterize his attendance as "sporadic," and no reason is given justifying the finding that it was "regular." This also ignores the Defense argument as to why he was there, which, if plausible, would undermine the Chamber's interpretation as the only plausible inference. Moving from attendance at meetings to activities involving evacuation and other potential crimes, the paragraph no longer names individuals but simply states that "the Standing Committee visited Battambang," "the Standing Committee decided to transfer 400,000," the "Standing Committee considered," etc. Individuals are not identified. Given that Khieu Samphan was not a member and that his role in the Standing Committee was heavily contested, the failure to specify in what way each of the Accused was involved in these visits or decisions is a glaring omission, likely based on the lack of evidence. JCE cannot make up for this lack of specific evidence because the findings so far have only shown that there was a policy of revolution that was embraced by both of the Accused along with other leaders, but it has not shown that the policy of evacuation was part of those policies or was intended by Khieu Samphan or that he participated in the decision-making process at all, let alone affirmatively.

As to Nuon Chea, in Paragraph 746 the Chamber acknowledges that there is no evidence that he participated in the visits or in the decisions, but they find that he is connected to them anyway based upon the importance of his role:

> The report concerning the Standing Committee's visit to the Northwest Zone does not indicate who attended. The Chamber notes however that NUON Chea was present in Cambodia in late August 1975, had ultimate decision-making authority, was a long-standing member of the Standing Committee, and played a central and ongoing role in the development of Party policy. Although there is no evidence that NUON Chea travelled with other members of the Standing Committee to the Northwest Zone in August 1975, the Chamber is satisfied that at the least he participated in developing and deciding upon the plans and policies reflected in the Standing Committee Report which followed this visit.[318]

The Chamber is "satisfied," but where is the evidence of his actual connection beyond an inference that because he was centrally involved in policy he participated in the decision? (How? What did he say? Did he object? What other inferences are plausible?) The absence of a reasoned weighing of the evidence, the Defense arguments, and of a justification of the inferences and findings is glaring. The only evidence cited (in footnote 2349) by the Chamber to ground this important finding is the general discussion of Nuon Chea's role in the prior section of the Judgment "Section 7; Roles and Functions, paras 313-317, 348." While the inference is not unreasonable, is it the only possible inference from the evidence? It is clearly not. The paragraphs cited in the footnote (313-317) add little except what his formal roles were. The key finding is in Paragraph 348, where the Judgment says the Chamber will follow the conclusions of experts Short and Chandler, that Pol Pot and Nuon Chea wielded ultimate decision-making authority in the Standing Committee. There is no detailed examination of the reasons given by Short and Chandler for their conclusion, nor is there any discussion of relevant Defense arguments on this matter. Even accepting that the conclusion is correct, how does it necessarily follow that a particular, specific decision made in connection with a Standing Committee visit to the provinces involved Nuon Chea?

The reasoning by which the Chamber affirms the connection of Khieu Samphan to this decision is even more tenuous.[319] It finds that he was in China during the visit of the Standing Committee. It further finds that, "There is no evidence that he took part directly in the planning that culminated in decisions issued in late August 1975."[320] The Chamber continues to find, however, that because of his economic authority, attendance at Standing Committee meetings, and his role in developing party policy for the socialist revolution, it is satisfied that he was notified of the decisions and what led up to them "soon after his return to Cambodia." The ability to infer the temporal dimension is particularly striking in the absence of *any* evidence cited. Moreover, the fact that he may have been "notified" would in fairness be overshadowed by the fact that, per the Chamber's own account, he was not consulted in regard to this very important decision. The Chamber again does not consider what other inferences are plausible. Would the Chamber's finding not seem to support an inference justifying the Defense contention that Khieu Samphan played no role in decision-making in the Standing Committee? The Chamber is again "satisfied" that he was notified, but again the Court's use of a passive narrative construction obscures by whom he was notified. In what manner and why? Who else was notified? Is "notified" the same as proactively "informed," or did he incidentally find out? These are very relevant questions, because the answers would bear directly upon whether there is evidence of a shared intent in regard to the crimes alleged.

Ensuing attempts to link Khieu Samphan to specific criminal conduct seem equally unconvincing. In Paragraph 757, the Chamber finds that on 2 November 1975 Khieu Samphan attended a Standing Committee meeting at which it was decided that Norodom Phurissara could not be trusted and was recalled from oversees. As to what happened to him, the Judgment states, "Former GRUNK ministers loyal to NORODOM Sihanouk and/or recalled from overseas, including NORODOM Phurissara, were later re-educated at Boeng Trabek, some disappearing."[321] How the fate of such individuals bears on Khieu Samphan is not made clear or even discussed. There is no discussion of what inferences can be drawn from the evidence.

Beyond stating that Khieu Samphan was at the meeting, the Judgment says nothing about the nature of his participation or if he even said anything or was asked his opinion. He was not yet even a full rights member of the Central Committee (that happened in January 1976). The fate of Norodom is not made clear in the text or in the accompanying footnote. The Judgment says "some disappeared," but does not state if Norodom was one of them or, if he was killed, when that decision was made or by whom. One is left wondering what this has to do with the individual responsibility of Khieu Samphan or, even more relevantly, with his membership of the JCE, which is the subject of this chapter of the Judgment. The paragraph goes on to say that Khieu Samphan lectured to returning intellectuals and in those lectures justified the evacuation policy. He also stated that the "knowledge" originating from colonialist education had to be destroyed. Advocating the destruction of colonial intellectual ideas was hardly novel or criminal, and was typical of all anti-colonialist struggles in the developing world. Again, it is not clear what conclusion the Chamber draws from these factual findings.

Although Chapter 14 of the Judgment is supposed to be establishing the way in which the Accused shared the common purpose of the JCE to implement socialist revolution through specific criminal policies, it is far from clear how much of the evidence adduced supports the conclusions the Judgment reaches in this regard. For example, in Paragraph 772 the Judgment states that, "Party leaders, including POL Pot, KHIEU Samphan and NUON Chea, led education sessions in Phnom Penh, beginning soon after 17 April 1975 and continuing throughout the DK era. They lectured Zone, Sector and District officials, as well as ordinary cadres, about the identification and elimination of enemies, continuation of the armed struggle…." This finding might indeed be relevant to Khieu Samphan's responsibility if the Judgment identified what specific education session he attended, what he said there and to whom, and whether he encouraged the violent elimination of enemies. Such detail is lacking. The typical phrase, "Party leaders, including … Khieu Sampan," masks the attribution of specific responsibility. We know already that the JCE aimed at socialist revolution in the post-April 1975 era. What needs to be specified for each of the Accused is that they shared a *criminal intent* to implement that revolution using criminal means alleged in the Closing Order to comprise the specific crimes against humanity enumerated. Despite the many factual findings, specific evidence and analysis is completely missing from this section of the Judgment in regard to Khieu Samphan.[322]

Having established what it apparently considers to be a sufficient foundation of factual findings on JCE, the Judgment then turns to "Legal Findings" in Chapter 14.1.5. In Paragraph 777, the Judgment finds in regard to the elements of the JCE that there is a plurality of persons who share an intent to implement a socialist revolution and defend the nation "by any means necessary." The Chamber does not state, however, that "any means necessary" encompasses the intent to use the crimes alleged in the Closing Order as the means to be employed. The Judgment includes Khieu Samphan and Nuon Chea in the group of 18 persons it names as constituting the members of the JCE. This finding is presumably based upon the preceding factual findings, but the specifics are not made clear as to Khieu Samphan. While it is fairly uncontroversial that he shared the intent to bring about a revolution, it is not at all clear how the Judgment attributes the intent to use "any means necessary" to him, or how it further attributes the intent to encompass the crimes charged within those means he allegedly intended.

There has, in fact, been no evidence whatsoever to ground this crucial qualification. The previous descriptions of Khieu Samphan in the "General Overview" and in the "Factual Findings," which do not weigh the evidence but merely narrate "facts," largely confine themselves to his advocacy of the revolution and do not present evidence or analysis as to with what criminal means he intended to accomplish this goal. By lumping all the 18 Khmer Rouge leaders together, the Judgment obscures to what extent Khieu Samphan as an individual shared the same intent as those who might have intended to use the charged crimes to implement their revolutionary purpose. There is thus a crucial step missing here: there might have been two groups, both of which agreed on the goal but disagreed on the means. This is where detailed analysis and weighing of the evidence pro and con is mandatory. That analysis has been missing in the conclusory narrative, which studiously refrains from specifying exactly what inferences are being drawn from the facts found. This is a serious failing of the liability assessment.

Population movement policy. The Trial Chamber's method of reaching findings without analyzing the relative weight of evidence or the inferences that may be drawn from it are unfortunately typical rather than exceptional. As the discussion moves ahead, Paragraph 748 references a September 1975 document that discusses the importance of "mass movement" in developing agricultural production.[323] Reflecting the difficulties the Chamber contended with at trial regarding admissibility of documentary evidence,[324] there is no evidence as to authorship of this document, and the Chamber acknowledges that the language of the document gives no indication of who was responsible for those policies or when they were decided. The Chamber nonetheless purports to definitively conclude that the document was the product of a meeting of the "Party leadership" sometime in September, and it finds (based only upon the general importance of his role) that Nuon Chea was present at this meeting.[325]

One is left to wonder what the Defense position on this point is as there is no reference to Defense arguments in any of the conclusions enumerated in these paragraphs.[326] This is a tenuous chain of inferences and suppositions backed by no reasoned analysis and weighing of the available evidence. According to the Judgment, there is a document of unknown provenance, and the document says nothing about where the policies referenced came from or who was involved in formulating them or when.[327] Yet the Chamber purports to be able to attribute this document to a specific meeting and to conclude that one of the Accused was there because he generally would have attended such meetings.[328] How such a conclusion meets the required standard and burden of proof remains unstated and is far from self-evident.

The only testimony cited about the formulation of the policy by the Party leadership is David Chandler, but the summary of his testimony, which the Judgment relies upon, hardly supports the specific findings as to the date and provenance of this particular document: "Finally, Expert David CHANDLER explained that the overall economic plan which emerged in late 1975 … was a product of the collective leadership of the Center, 'centred at some point in the Central Committee.'"[329] It turns out, however, that Chandler was not referencing the document in question in his testimony. So, can this testimony really bear the weight of the Chamber's finding that this document, *not mentioned by Chandler,* was the product of a meeting in September that Nuon Chea attended? And what was his input into this document? Chandler is vague not only as to timing but also as to who was involved, and he attributes the policy formulated in "late 1975" to the Central Committee, not to the Standing Committee. When individual responsibility is at stake, the problem of attribution to "collective leadership" is manifest here as well.

The Judgment does conclude that, in regard to Khieu Samphan, the Chamber cannot confirm his attendance because he was outside the country for part of September.[330] Astonishingly, however, it nonetheless attributes responsibility to him for the policy in that specific document, formulated, on its finding, when he was out of the country.[331] The basis of this attribution is that the Chamber recalls its previous findings that Khieu Samphan was "generally invited" to attend meetings about "the development of the country," that he "attended meetings" in 1974 where evacuations were "discussed," and that he also attended meetings in April-May 1975 where economic development was "addressed." On this basis, he is held to be responsible for a policy document of unknown authorship and purportedly the product of a policy meeting that he did not attend, and which may or may not have been related to the document. This finding is also reached in the absence of evidence that when Khieu Samphan did attend meetings, he participated in policy formation and decisions on all issues discussed.

It is tenuous enough to infer that someone was at a specific meeting because they generally attended meetings (which in the case of Khieu Samphan was never proved), but this finding also involves attribution of responsibility for a policy decision. What is telling is that none of the three examples given by the Chamber indicates that Khieu Samphan ever had such a role in *any* of the meetings he is cited as attending. In regard to the first meeting, the Judgment only says he was "invited"—hardly indicative of policy authority. At the other two meetings, it only says he attended, and the description indicates that matters were discussed but not decided. The Judgment is silent about his role at such meetings. It is thus a considerable leap to attribute this policy document to him, let alone to say that his responsibility has been proved beyond a reasonable doubt. Where is the testing of the evidence as to other permissible inferences?

The Chamber seems here to be grasping at straws to link Khieu Samphan to specific decisions that have criminal implications, as opposed to the role described in most of the "General Overview" and in this section, which consists mainly of his affirmation of ideological generalities about the revolution. Surely one quite reasonable inference is that, due to the nature of his political role, Khieu Samphan was generally invited to attend some meetings because it was important he was aware of the policies that the decision-makers were developing in order to explain and represent them in New York, Beijing, and elsewhere.

Subsequent paragraphs seek, but fail, to buttress the Trial Chamber's factual findings. Paragraph 752 states that in October the Standing Committee "assigned" Khieu Samphan the role of dealing with accounting, pricing, etc. This, however, again indicates that his role was limited to economic matters, as the Chamber had itself acknowledged when it concluded that his portfolio was largely limited to trade and economy. In Paragraph 753, it tries to link Khieu Samphan to the production target of three tons of rice per hectare by referencing the decision of an Economic Congress described in Revolutionary Flag. The only problem is that, as the Judgment acknowledges, there is no evidence that this Congress ever actually took place.[332] This inconvenient fact poses little difficulty for the Chamber, however, for it finds that the "policy document" cited above was consistent with this policy and with the resolution later published as a result of this "alleged First Nationwide Economics Congress," and can thus be attributed not only to the "Party leadership" but also to Khieu Samphan. There is no footnote here and the Judgment cites no evidence or reasoning whatsoever to ground this finding that Khieu Samphan was specifically involved and responsible for this policy, attributed to decisions made at a meeting which may never have happened. In a trial where the standard of proof is "beyond a reasonable doubt," such vagueness and uncertainty are supposed to be resolved in favor of the Accused (as the Chamber itself acknowledged in its general recitation of the principles for reviewing evidence), but time and time again, when confronting multiple plausible inferences, the Chamber glosses over this fact and adopts factual findings aligned with convicting the Accused.

This lack of precision and analytical deficiency runs through the entire section on population movements during the Khmer Rouge. In Paragraph 785, for example, the vagueness arises in regard to a crucial matter: the Court says that Khieu Samphan and Nuon Chea have stated that "*the Party was aware that people would sacrifice and face hardship*" (emphasis added) as a result of the population movement policy. The Court concludes from this that Nuon Chea and Khieu Samphan "both believed that the priority was building and defending the country." The problem here is that the Judgment does not explain how this is relevant to the charges against the Accused via the JCE. In the first statement they find that "the Party" was aware. "The Party" is an abstraction and is not on trial. The second statement is also hardly conclusive because "sacrifice and hardship" are normal in time of war and crisis, and such statements are typical of war leaders. The allegation of the JCE is based on a shared intent to build and defend the country, but that is not criminal and is an entirely legitimate political aim. Again, none of these statements shows that at the time of the alleged crimes the Accused said or did anything that showed their shared intent to use the charged criminal acts as the intended means to achieve legitimate goals. This paragraph is also redundant with previous overviews and findings about their political aims and the aims of the CPK.[333]

Repeating what has been already found in various parts of the Judgment, the Chamber then concludes that in 1974 and April 1975 the "Party leadership" decided to prioritize population transfer. The collective abstraction again detracts from the attribution of individual responsibility. The "Party leadership" is not a person on trial. Yet this entire key paragraph uses "the Party leadership" or similar abstractions as the subject.[334] A little later in the same Section, the Judgment concludes: "Over the course of the DK era, Zone secretaries and officials reported to POL Pot, NUON Chea, VORN Vet, SON Sen, Doeun and/or Office 870 on population movements, sometimes requesting further instructions."[335] Khieu Samphan is not mentioned at all in this finding, and because Nuon Chea is lumped together with the others and with Office 870, his individual role, beyond having heard some reports over the span of the entire Khmer Rouge era, is obscured.

These crucial findings again assume that the "Party" is collectively unified by a common purpose. Yet ensuing paragraphs of the Judgment give indications to the contrary. Although the Judgment has consistently treated the "Party leadership" as a monolithic block, the legal finding in Paragraph 807 makes clear that it was not. Mentioning the meetings that took place in 1974 and April 1975 where the Court finds the evacuation decision was made, the Judgment's description indicates a shifting cast of characters and an inability to be precise about who said what and when, and who was ultimately responsible for the actual decisions. The conclusion, after mentioning many individuals involved in these various meetings, states that, "The Chamber is therefore satisfied that the crimes committed during movement of population (phase one) can be imputed to various participants in the JCE including, at least, some Central and Standing Committee members such as POL Pot, Ta Mok, SON Sen, SAO Phim, VORN Vet and KOY Thuon." Strikingly, *neither* of the Accused is mentioned in this list, yet in the legal conclusions specific to each of the Accused, these crimes are ultimately imputed to both Nuon Chea and Khieu Samphan.[336]

The discussion of the JCE encompassing "Phase Two" of the population movements is even vaguer in regard to attribution.[337] The Judgment states that instructions from the "Centre" were passed to Zone and Autonomous Region commanders. From this, it concludes:

> The Chamber is therefore satisfied that transfers from the Southwest, West, East and Central (old North) Zones to the Northwest and Central (old North) Zones, Sectors 103 and 505, as well as within the Northwest, East and Central (old North) Zones, can be imputed to participants in the JCE including, at least, some members of the Central and Standing Committees, government ministers, and Zone and Autonomous Sector secretaries, such as VORN Vet, MEY Prang, SON Sen, KOY Thuon, KE Pauk, CHANN Sam, CHOU Chet, Ta Mok, ROS Nhim, SAO Phim, BOU Phat, YONG Yem and BORN Nan.[338]

This language hardly confirms a monolithic leadership structure with a fixed JCE membership, all of whom intended to accomplish the revolution by specific criminal means, such as the specified transfers. And again, neither Nuon Chea nor Khieu Samphan is named here. How does that comport with the view of their centrality in CPK decision-making and policy formulation as articulated in earlier parts of the

Judgment? These sections of findings on how the decisions were made seem to undermine the Judgment's earlier findings in regard to collective decision-making, as well as the foundation of its finding that there was a JCE that encompassed all of these individuals they discuss in regard to all of the crimes alleged in the Closing Order.

Killings at Tuol Po Chrey. In regard to the killings at Tuol Po Chrey, the factual findings that form the basis for the JCE connection are, if anything, even more tenuous.[339] The Chamber reasons:

> [A]lthough executions at Tuol Po Chrey are not explicitly linked to the Targeting Policy in the Closing Order, they are an example of the general pattern of targeting Khmer Republic officials identified under the Targeting Policy. Taking into account the nature of the charges concerning the executions at Tuol Po Chrey, the Accused therefore had adequate notice of them. Within the scope of Case 002/01, the Chamber will consider whether, with regard to the Targeting Policy, a JCE existed which resulted in the commission of the crimes of murder and extermination at Tuol Po Chrey.[340]

Here, the Chamber has basically admitted that there is no evidence that the murders at Tuol Po Chrey are encompassed within the shared intent of the JCE members to use these crimes to implement their common purpose. The language stating that the Accused were "on notice" clearly suggests that the Accused did not intend the crimes, but rather that perhaps the crimes were foreseeable to them. With this language, the Chamber has moved toward an application of JCE III, which it is in fact barred from doing by the 2010 Pre-Trial Chamber decision that found JCE III had not yet been established in customary international law in 1975-1979.[341] If the Chamber is to remain properly within the parameters of JCE I, then either the Accused were part of the group that shared the intent to use systematic murder of officials as a way of implementing the socialist revolution or they were not. If it cannot be proved beyond a reasonable doubt that they were, then they were not members of a JCE plurality, and cannot be held constructively liable for the crimes committed by other members of such a group.

The ensuing paragraphs deal with findings bearing on this issue.[342] They again take the form of a narrative, rather than an analysis that carefully weighs the evidence for and against and considers what reasonable inferences may be drawn. Again, the evidence connecting Khieu Samphan is particularly weak. The first piece of evidence cited is a 2011 statement that Nuon Chea made, asserting that, "Communism mandates the elimination of those who pose threats to the country ..."[343] It is not at all clear from the text how the Chamber believes this 2011 statement bears upon the intent of Nuon Chea vis-à-vis a policy that was allegedly formulated according to a shared purpose in 1975. As for Khieu Samphan, the first connection cited for him is that, "Both KHIEU Samphan and IENG Sary maintained that the people and cadres had a deep hatred of Khmer Republic leaders, knew of their 'true nature' and were therefore constantly on 'revolutionary alert.'"[344] The Chamber does not explain how being on "revolutionary alert" proves Khieu Samphan's intention to participate in a policy of systematic murder of Khmer Republic officials.

The next piece of evidence (again narrated and not analyzed at all) is that in a June 1974 meeting of the Central Committee, attended by Khieu Samphan and Nuon Chea, the executions at Oudong "were discussed."[345] There is no mention by whom, what was said, or whether it was approved as a future policy or merely reported, let alone what Khieu Samphan or Nuon Chea specifically said, if they said anything at all.[346] There is, again, sloppiness in the factual basis of the narrative, as revealed by examining footnote 2573, the *sole source* cited. This footnote merely references Paragraphs 143-147 of the earlier "General Overview." In that passage, it appears that the "plan" that was affirmed in the April 1975 meeting was for the evacuation of Phnom Penh, and there is no reference in those paragraphs to approval of a policy of murder. Moreover, the evidence as to what happened at that meeting and who attended was heavily contested by both Defense teams, as it was based on the testimony of a single witness, and it was not at all clear how he could have heard what he claimed to hear simply by being "in the vicinity" of the meeting.[347] In those referenced paragraphs (143-147) there was, as typical of many parts of the Judgment, no serious examination of the arguments for and against this evidence or careful analysis of the credibility of this key witness. The matter is dealt with in a few lines in a footnote.

Notwithstanding these glaring inadequacies, based on the evidence just reviewed, Paragraph 817 finds that there was "overwhelming evidence" of a targeting policy "by the Party leadership." Khieu Samphan is not mentioned at all in the narrative of the evidence supporting this finding, and Nuon Chea's name only appears as one of the individuals to whom "some of" the reports of killings were "addressed or copied." Paragraph 818 deals with the dissemination of this policy and Khieu Samphan is again not even mentioned. Nuon Chea appears only as one who gave instruction on how to tell enemies from friends. The significance of having reports "addressed or copied" to one is not analyzed in terms of what inferences can be drawn in regard to these reports. In which cases was the report addressed as opposed to copied to the Accused? Is this distinction important? How many other people were the reports addressed or copied to? Why were the reports addressed or copied to these people, and how does Nuon Chea figure into that group? While one can well surmise what his role may have been, surmise does not constitute legal analysis and it certainly does not provide the basis for proof beyond a reasonable doubt. [348]

Building upon the conclusions just discussed, Paragraphs 835-836 provide the legal findings arising from this narrative of policy and pattern. The conclusion is, again, that there was a JCE that had a common purpose of socialist revolution and that was not criminal in purpose, but that "the policies formulated by the Khmer Rouge involved the commission of a crime as a means of bringing the common plan to fruition."[349] It should be noted that there is no finding that the policies were criminal, or that criminal policies were encompassed within the common plan as the intended means of implementation. Rather, the finding is that those policies "involved" a crime as a means of achieving the revolution. The further finding is that "there was a policy to target former Khmer Republic officials which involved the murder and extermination of former Khmer Republic officials at Tuol Po Chrey." So, "a crime" becomes two crimes: murder and extermination. The policy is not to murder or exterminate, but rather to eliminate enemies to the revolution, and that policy in some unspecified way "involves" these crimes. In the opinion of the Chamber that is enough to make murder and extermination of enemies an intended means encompassed within the common purpose of revolution. This finding, moreover, is only directed at "the Party" as a monolithic abstraction. The connection between the intent of the specific Accused and the JCE comes in the following section, where the Chamber closes the loop on its deeply troubled liability assessment, applying its misunderstanding of the applicable law to a vague and ill-proven body of factual findings, with predictably disastrous results.

Poor Application of Law to Facts

As detailed above, throughout the liability assessment, the Chamber relies on a flimsy presumption that all decisions made by the Khmer Rouge leadership were made on such a basis that responsibility for the decisions could be attributed to the Accused in the absence of actual evidence indicating specific participation. The Court tends to draw broad inculpatory inferences about both Accused from their mere presence (or in some instances just *inferred* presence) at particular political meetings. The ECCC's legal conclusions here are completely out of step with the leading jurisprudence of other international tribunals, such as the ICTY, where Judges have considered similar types of evidence and concluded that mere presence does not necessarily imply a shared intent or common purpose in the case of a JCE.[350] This approach also fails to provide a sufficient basis for proving *de facto* authority over specific groups of perpetrators—an essential element of Superior Responsibility.

Nuon Chea liability pursuant to JCE

While the previous chapter dealt with JCE in general, referring to the 18 alleged members of the JCE and only occasionally referencing the Accused specifically, Chapter 15 focuses specifically on the liability of Nuon Chea, citing charges from the Closing Order that Nuon Chea committed various crimes "through a JCE." The first section of Chapter 15 is entitled "Knowledge Relevant to the Modes of Liability." (15.1). Yet, when the Judgment turns to the analysis of Nuon Chea's specific liability under JCE in this section, it reverts impermissibly to a JCE III rationale. Instead of focusing on the crucial issue of what was the common purpose and shared intent that defined the JCE, the Court focuses on *awareness and knowledge of a likelihood that crimes would be, had been, or were being committed*:

> Therefore, in this section, the Chamber will examine whether, prior to the commission of the crimes falling within the scope of Case 002/01, the Accused was aware of the substantial likelihood of their later occurrence (Section 15.1.1), and whether the Accused had knowledge of the crimes concurrent with (Section 15.1.2) or after their commission (Section 15.1.3).[351]

Despite the fact that "substantial likelihood of commission" is *not* a basis for liability under JCE I, Paragraph 840 concludes that because Nuon Chea planned for the revolution to rely on peasants, the only reasonable expectation on his part was that massive numbers of serious crimes would be committed during the forced evacuations. The paragraph concludes that he knew "there was a substantial likelihood" that the crimes would be committed. This issue of awareness and foreseeability of risk could hypothetically bear upon Superior Responsibility liability for the Accused, but in Paragraph 846 it becomes clear that the focus of the Judgment here is on JCE, where the Chamber states that because the crimes charged formed "consistent patterns of conduct" and because of his access to information, the only reasonable inference is that Nuon Chea was aware of the substantial likelihood that the "implementation of plans to evacuate the urban areas" would result in the commission of the crimes charged.[352] One must also recall here that even if JCE III were a permitted mode of liability, the existence of a JCE III depends upon prior establishment of a basic JCE (JCE I) defined by the required shared intent.

The fairly lengthy treatment of Nuon Chea's role and his knowledge are documented almost solely by references to the previous sections on Joint Criminal Enterprise. On this basis, the Judgment concludes that he played a role in the formulation and implementation of the policies constituting the JCE, but as we saw, those previous sections were often vague in their analysis of the role of individuals as opposed to the party leadership or other abstract entities. Above all, what remains unexplained is why these crucial sections focus on establishing the foreseeability of the commission of the crimes when that is an element of JCE III but not of JCE I. One would have expected the Chamber to focus on evidence establishing that Nuon Chea shared the *criminal intent* that would have defined the JCE I.

The validity of the Chamber's construction of JCE is further impugned in its treatment of Nuon Chea's alleged responsibility for the killings at Tuol Po Chrey.[353] Here the Judgment explicitly states that

"Although there is no evidence that he knew of the specific nature" of these crimes, he knew of an "ongoing pattern" of targeting Khmer Republic officials. They reason that because he knew that cities like Pursat were to be evacuated, he also knew that such executions occurred. Apart from the rather tenuous logical reasoning in this passage, the Chamber's analysis ignores the fact that to prove Nuon Chea's membership in the JCE and the connection of the JCE to these crimes, it is the common purpose—the shared intent—that is alone dispositive, not whether he had *knowledge* that crimes were being committed. In response to the Defense's contention that it was the Zones who were responsible for the implementation of the evacuations (Section 15.2), the Chamber finds that this is true, but concludes nonetheless that the "Party, including Nuon Chea, relied upon the Zones" for implementation.[354] This is again problematic from the standpoint of proving JCE, because the analysis stops short of expressly connecting the finding to the question of *intent* of the members of the JCE plurality.

In Paragraph 863, the Judgment finally turns to "planning the common purpose." Unfortunately, these crucial sections consist of a narrative that simply cites back to the earlier sections on JCE and the "Historical Background." The focus returns again to the "socialist revolution," as the Judgment argues that the Party's plan to implement the revolution involved relocating up to 500,000 people. Relying on the discussion of his role, the Chamber concludes that Nuon Chea was "aware of and supported" this plan for relocation. The Chamber does not use the word "intent" to link him to the plan. It concludes by saying that through his role he "not only shared support for the common plan, but played a key role in formulating its content."[355]

While this sentence refers to the common plan, it states that Nuon Chea "supported" it, which could imply that he aided and abetted the JCE rather than that he was a member of it. The Judgment again lacks precision on key elements. It is only in the conclusion of the JCE section on Nuon Chea that the Chamber returns to the language of the elements it sets out in the applicable law section early in the Judgment and properly states them.[356] Thus, it concludes that on the basis of the foregoing analysis, he "shared the intent of the other members of the JCE to bring about the common purpose through implementation of the Party's policies on population movements and targeting Khmer Republic officials."[357]

This sudden pivot in rhetorical formulation is striking, for as we saw throughout the "foregoing analysis," the mental element connecting Nuon Chea to the alleged targeting policy was "knowledge" of such crimes and awareness of a substantial risk that they would be committed. Neither of these is an adequate basis in itself to establish the requisite *mens rea* for this JCE I. There is a manifest inconsistency here between the actual findings in Paragraph 846[358] and the reformulation found in this ultimate conclusion, where it is for the first time argued that he intended to bring about these killings. Even more strikingly, the Judgment goes on to abruptly conclude that Nuon Chea also shared the intent with other JCE members to commit murder and other inhumane acts during the population movements, as well as to commit murder and extermination at Tuol Po Chrey.[359]

In regard to the killings that occurred during the population movements, it must be recalled that the previous sections of this chapter on Nuon Chea merely concluded that he was aware of the "substantial likelihood" that such crimes would be committed. This in no way supports the conclusion in Paragraph 876 that he intended for them to be committed as part of the shared purpose of the JCE. The same issue arises from the conclusion that the Court's analysis shows that he intended for murder and extermination to be committed at Tuol Po Chrey as part of the JCE. One wonders if the conclusions and the preceding analyses were written by two different persons because they do not share the same legal language and the conclusions, particularly in regard to the inclusion of the killings within the common purpose of the JCE, are simply not supported by the Chamber's own factual findings in earlier sections. Those sections, as we saw, were deeply analytically flawed. But even if we assume those conclusions were well-founded, there remains a glaring gap between the findings in those sections and the general conclusion on Nuon Chea's JCE liability reached here.[360]

Nuon Chea's liability pursuant to Superior Responsibility

Turning to Superior Responsibility analysis for Nuon Chea, the Chamber correctly identifies "effective control" as required for establishing the superior-subordinate relationship as a required element of Superior Responsibility. Under the currently prevailing jurisprudence on Superior Responsibility, in order to establish liability, it must be shown beyond a reasonable doubt that the specific individual Accused stood in a superior-subordinate relationship to the specific perpetrators of a specific crime. As the *Kunarac* Trial Chamber found at the ICTY, it must also be shown that the alleged subordinates recognized the Accused as their superior at the actual time when the crimes were committed.[361] In Case 002/01, the dearth of specific evidence about the substance of high-level meetings posed significant difficulties for the Chamber in establishing the key element of "effective control" necessary to prove the superior-subordinate relationship. Instead, the Chamber appears to rely upon general findings that authority was concentrated in certain bodies such as the Standing Committee, or sometimes, more vaguely, in "the CPK" or "the CPK leadership."[362] Such a finding, however, is legally insufficient to ground a conclusion of the existence of a superior-subordinate relationship and effective control.

The Trial Chamber defines effective control in regard to Nuon Chea as follows: "Superior responsibility depends upon an Accused's ability to exercise effective control over subordinates, that is the actual power to take reasonable and necessary measures to prevent or punish the crimes."[363] According to the Closing Order and as relevant to Case 002/01, "Nuon Chea is responsible as a superior and exercised effective control over the Revolutionary Army of Kampuchea (RAK), Zone, Sector and District Committee members, local militia and cadre."[364] As discussed earlier, the Chamber's definition does not necessarily reflect the state of what was in 1975 still called "command responsibility."[365] In fact, this precise definition of effective control as the power to prevent or punish is not current in the definitions from 1945-1975, but is rather the formulation that was adopted by the ICTY and subsequent tribunals. Be that as it may, under the Chamber's decision, the crucial issue is on what basis the status of Nuon Chea as a superior with command authority is established in regard to the named entities.

In the few short paragraphs in which the Chamber satisfies itself that the required superior-subordinate relationship exists, the central problem is that it does not employ the "actual power … to prevent or punish" standard that it just articulated. Another equally serious problem is that there is no consideration of the Defense case on this point. The findings are just set out as obvious facts requiring little discussion, analysis, or weighing of conflicting arguments and evidence. This is surprising, given the murky nature of central elements of the Khmer Rouge structures of authority as revealed and acknowledged in the earlier parts of the Judgment. One would have at least expected a consideration of whether all of the available evidence—full of contradictions, opacities, and lacunae as it is—admits more than one reasonable inference. An examination of the evidence and standard relied upon by the Judgment in finding beyond a reasonable doubt that Nuon Chea bears Superior Responsibility reveals the fragility of the conclusion.

The Chamber, in fact, bases its conclusion largely on one short paragraph, consisting of three sentences, and which we will consider in its entirety.[366] The first point made states that, "Along with POL

Pot, the only person who was officially senior to him, NUON Chea exercised ultimate decision-making power." This in itself is not dispositive because ultimate power in making political decisions does not necessarily translate into direct *de facto* command authority over security and military entities and others who are direct perpetrators of the crimes charged. The paragraph relies on only two further points to support its conclusion.

The next sentence states that, "Although Khmer Rouge forces attacking Phnom Penh were under the direct control of the Zones, not the Party Centre, in the lead up to 1975, Khmer Rouge forces executed a number of orders from the CPK leadership, including from Nuon Chea, to attack and forcibly transfer the inhabitants of the cities upon their capture." This sentence reveals several glaring weaknesses in its capacity to support the Chamber's findings. First, the phrase "in the lead up to 1975" indicates that this sentence refers to events in a period outside the jurisdiction of the ECCC, not to the relevant period. Whether or not Nuon Chea had *de facto* authority at one period does not establish that he continued to have that authority at the time when the crimes charged were committed. The fact that he had high *de jure* positions in the Party is also not relevant to the legal questions of his *de facto* authority at that time. To this end, it is noteworthy that the Chamber itself found that it was unable to conclude that he was a member of the Military Committee.

Second, one cannot read the sentence without wondering about the legal significance of the acknowledgement that the relevant forces were "under the direct control of the Zones not the Party Centre." This is a key element in the Defense case and requires discussion, but the analysis one would expect from a well-reasoned legal opinion is entirely absent here. It is incumbent upon the trier of fact to ask fundamental questions about the nature of the actual authority of the Accused. If the Zones controlled these forces, then through what mechanisms and in what manner did Nuon Chea possess and exercise effective control over the Zones? What is the evidence that he possessed *de facto* authority over the specific units and at the specific time that the alleged crimes were committed? This would be required by the standard applied, for example in the *Kunarac* Trial Judgment referenced above. The necessary evidence is missing here, and the footnotes refer only to previous sections of the Judgment, which, as is apparent to anyone who conducts a thorough reading of the text, do not contain the required evidentiary detail or legal analysis.

Finally, the critical allegation in this sentence is that the "Khmer Rouge forces" executed orders from the "CPK leadership, including NUON Chea," to carry out attacks. However, no details are provided about any specific orders, what individual signed or communicated them, specific attacks, or which forces carried them out. If the footnotes provided these details that would lend some weight to the conclusions, but they do not provide the necessary detail. The footnotes only contain general references to previous sections of the Judgment, none of which provide the crucial evidentiary details, survey the relevant Defense arguments, or conduct a more rigorous legal analysis. The conclusion here, even apart from the temporal reference to pre-1975, is vague and general. This does not meet the requirement, made clear in a long line of ICTY cases, that a Superior Responsibility conviction be based upon specific proof beyond a reasonable doubt of *de facto* authority over the specific units who carried out the crimes alleged. The further problem here is that we have seen how the previous sections of the Judgment rely upon attribution to abstract entities such as the "CPK leadership," but what is required here is specific evidence of Nuon Chea's personal *de facto* authority.

The final sentence of this crucial paragraph merely alleges that "in early April 1975, Zone and other officials reported to 'senior leaders,' including Nuon Chea on their progress in advancing on Phnom Penh." This sentence, with no supporting details, may not be entirely irrelevant, but it is hardly dispositive and would require much greater factual elaboration and analysis. In what sense did the officials "report"? Was this an informational briefing to political leaders? Was it a formal report of the *de facto* military authorities informing the civilian authorities of the military operations they had decided upon and were implementing? Or was it the reporting of field commanders to their superiors? These questions remain unaddressed.

What is also entirely missing from this paragraph is a reference to whether or not Nuon Chea personally could have prevented the crimes from occurring or could have punished those who committed them. This is required by the definition of effective control as "the power to prevent or punish." Although the Chamber has correctly articulated this as the definition of "effective control," it adduces no evidence and engages in no analysis on this point. In fact, Paragraph 894 does not include the words "prevent" or "punish" or any associated synonyms. Although a later section (5.1.4.5.3) concludes that he did not make an attempt to prevent the crimes or to punish the perpetrators, there has been no specific finding that he in fact possessed the power to do so as the criterion for *de facto* authority.

Paragraph 894 begins with a conclusion: "In view of the foregoing [i.e. Par. 893], the Chamber is satisfied that the most senior CPK members, including NUON Chea, played a key role in ordering particular attacks …" This sentence is again vague as to Nuon Chea's personal authority as an alleged superior. He is lumped together again with the general "senior CPK members" without any reference to his personal role or authority. Yet Superior Responsibility is an attribute attaching to an individual, in order to ground his or her liability for acts committed by subordinates under his or her effective control.

Here, however, the Chamber's conclusion does not state that he ordered these attacks, but rather that this group of individuals "played a key role" in doing so. What does it mean to play a "key role" in ordering? Who actually issued the orders? Were they general policies or specific orders? If specific, who signed or transmitted them? Who drafted them? These facts and many others remain entirely obscure, and thus this "conclusion" may "satisfy" the Chamber, but it most certainly does not establish the personal *de facto* authority and effective control of Nuon Chea over the relevant forces. The underlying problem is that the Chamber has not previously made factual findings that can fill in the necessary details and answer the required questions. The fact that the Judges are struggling to cope with a complex and in many ways inadequate evidentiary basis for this issue does not obviate the need for them to meet the required standard of proof, no matter what one possible set of inferences may indicate to them about Nuon Chea's role.

The only remaining support adduced by the Chamber for its conclusion on the crucial element of the superior-subordinate relationship is the following sentence: "The Chamber accepts the view of Expert Phillip SHORT that, 'it would not have been possible for Zone commanders to act against or outside the *broad policy consensus* that had been laid down by the Centre.'"[367] (emphasis added) The Court then immediately concludes, "Accordingly, the Chamber finds that a *de facto* superior-subordinate relationship existed between NUON Chea and both the Zone secretaries and military commanders in 1975."[368] How this conclusion is supported by the quotation from Short is not explained. His statement refers to a "broad policy consensus" of the Center. This has no bearing on the issue of whether Nuon Chea possessed the power to prevent or punish in regard to the specific perpetrators of specific crimes.

The jurisprudence of the ICTY developed in a manner that applied a strict standard to the proof required to establish the superior-subordinate relationship. In cases such as *Celebici, Kvocka, Blaskic, Kunarac*, and others, specific proof of the essential element of effective control was held to be required in regard to the specific units that committed specific crimes. What the Chamber here seems to be doing, as revealed by the ultimate quotation from Short, is to simply infer *de facto* authority from political and policy leadership, and apply that inference to the entire senior leadership of the Khmer Rouge, sometimes referred to as the "Centre" and sometimes to the CPK's "senior members." A more legitimate approach to establishing Nuon Chea's responsibility under this theory of liability would have involved the Trial Chamber conducting a detailed, substantive, and precise analysis of the personal role of the Accused, and the scope of his personal authority in regard to specific allegedly subordinate personnel who were responsible for the commission of the crimes. [369] In one final, strange twist, despite the lengthy analysis concluding that Nuon Chea was responsible as a superior for the crimes alleged in the Closing Order, the Chamber does not actually enter a conviction against him on this basis, relying instead on JCE as the primary theory of responsibility.[370] However, the Judgment states that it will take its Superior Responsibility conclusions into account in sentencing.

Khieu Samphan liability pursuant to JCE

In regard to Khieu Samphan, the Chamber finds that there was insufficient evidence to establish his responsibility as a superior.[371] Accordingly, it chooses again to rely on JCE as the primary theory of responsibility. In Paragraphs 961-962, the Chamber summarizes its previous findings in regard to the political role of Khieu Samphan, citing only those sections of the Judgment which, as detailed above, were far from conclusive in regard to his role at the policy level. Paragraphs 962 and 963 conclude that because of his various roles and his public statements endorsing the general policies "to build and defend the country according to the Party line," Khieu Samphan was a member of the JCE responsible for the commission of the crimes alleged in the indictment. What specific evidence is cited in ensuing paragraphs to demonstrate that he shared the common purpose to commit these crimes of murder, extermination, persecution, and so on?

The overarching problem with this section of the Judgment is that it does not cite specific evidence, but merely sets out a series of conclusory statements and cites previous sections of the Judgment, which purportedly established the key facts beyond a reasonable doubt. The foregoing analysis of the Judgment's findings in regard to Khieu Samphan's attendance, participation, and role at policy-level meetings indicated the uncertainties surrounding both what exactly transpired at those meetings and what Khieu Samphan may or may not have contributed to those few it can be proved he attended. In a number of cases it was seen that the Judgment acknowledged some of these gaps and uncertainties. Yet in this section of the Judgment, arguing that Khieu Samphan is to be held responsible as a member of a JCE that intended to commit these crimes, the crucial paragraphs grounding Khieu Samphan's participation contain no detailed analysis of that evidence, no acknowledgement of the uncertainties previously referenced, and no analytical weighing of the Defense and Prosecution arguments. What we find instead is paragraph after paragraph of conclusory statements, sweeping in their scope and generality, justified only by footnotes that reference page numbers of a previous narrative section of the Judgment devoted to the role and function of the CPK leaders in general.

In many of these paragraphs, Khieu Samphan is simply lumped together with "the Party leaders" of the CPK as responsible for various policies and aware of their implementation. This is very unsophisticated analysis, as the evidence adduced by the Chamber, as well as other evidence before the Court, clearly indicates that "Party leaders" were not a monolithic block. Moreover, the law demands that Khieu Samphan's role must be distinguished from this grouping and particularized, based on factual findings, in order to establish his individual liability. A few examples, representative of this entire section of the Judgment may suffice to demonstrate this point.

In Paragraph 952, in the section tellingly entitled "Awareness of the Substantial Likelihood of the Commission of the Crimes,"[372] the Chamber states that Khieu Samphan knew that there were food shortages throughout the country. The Judgment immediately goes on to conclude that, "Party leaders, including Khieu Samphan, nonetheless planned forced population movements …. These plans therefore inevitably contemplated and involved the crimes that would later be committed."[373] The only factual references cited to support this key conclusion are Paragraphs 576, 604-606, and 1023-1029. Khieu Samphan's name does not appear in Paragraph 576, which refers only to "the Party," and the paragraph states that the "Party leadership believed that population movements allowed it to overcome challenges in building and defending in the country." In Paragraphs 604-606, Khieu Samphan is mentioned twice. The first reference states that he was present at a meeting where it was reported that in regard to rice production, "30 percent of the 1976 goal had already been reached and attributed this success to careful and detailed planning."[374]

The second reference to Khieu Samphan states that he was present at a "Health and Social Affairs meeting" at which the Party leadership "reiterated that unless three tonnes per hectare were achieved, the party would not be able to feed the people or defend the country."[375] There is no evidence cited as to what Khieu Samphan said or did, if anything, at these meetings. Neither of these references indicates any connection to criminal conduct or participation in a common criminal purpose. The content of these three paragraphs from the previous factual findings part of the Judgment in no way supports the sweeping conclusion as to Khieu Samphan's alleged role and criminal intent in the JCE attributed to "the Party leaders" in Paragraph 952. The remaining paragraphs (1023-1029) also contain no discussion of specific evidence or findings because they come from the concluding section, "The Criminal Responsibility of Khieu Samphan," which merely states general conclusions from the preceding sections of the Judgment. In other words, there is no apparent evidentiary basis cited in Paragraph 952 to support the attribution of criminal intent to Khieu Samphan that is alleged there.

Paragraph 952, however, does not end with the allegation of shared criminal intent with the "Party leaders." As in Paragraph 951 and other parts of this section of the Judgment, it concludes that because of his alleged participation in planning the crimes, his attendance at "instructional meetings" and his access to the Khmer Rouge magazines, "Khieu Samphan knew of the substantial likelihood that these plans and policies to move people between rural areas … would result in the commission of the crimes during phase two." As indicated above, JCE I must be established by a showing of a common purpose that encompasses the alleged crimes. That common purpose cannot be established by arguing that the commission of such crimes was foreseeable because of an awareness of a substantial likelihood that they might be committed. That is the province of JCE III, which is outside the jurisdiction of the Tribunal. Nonetheless, as indicated by the title of Section 16.1.1, the argument of "awareness of a substantial likelihood" is the foundational ground for holding Khieu Samphan liable. The Chamber thus appears, as argued above, to be bringing JCE III by the back door because of the evidentiary weakness in demonstrating Khieu Samphan's participation in the common purpose by reference to his words, deeds, and conduct. Paragraph 952 provides another example of the way in which a shallow evidentiary base in previous parts of the Judgment is amplified by conclusory statements that do not follow from the evidence cited, and which are then transformed into support for Khieu Samphan's participation in the JCE via his alleged awareness that crimes might be committed during the implementation of the Khmer Rouge policies.

To take a further example, the key section entitled "Policy Meetings: Planning the Common Purpose"[376] contains general statements that Khieu Samphan attended various meetings. On this basis the Judgment concludes, "The Chamber is therefore satisfied that his attendance at meetings and his contribution to plans of the Party Centre demonstrate that he not only shared the common purpose" to evacuate urban areas and target Khmer Republic officials, "but that he also played a key role in formulating the content of the common purpose and policies."[377]

No specific evidence is cited that grounds these conclusions. Neither does the Trial Chamber offer any analysis of that evidence in regard to the burden of proof (which is virtually never mentioned in this entire part of the Judgment). As already noted, the evidence as to Khieu Samphan's role in regard to policy formulation, and as to what he actually said and did at meetings he attended, was practically non-existent. Evidence the Chamber did review on this subject was highly contestable. The conclusions stating that he attended meetings are not specific as to what he said or did at the meetings that would prove beyond a reasonable doubt that he shared the criminal common purpose of the alleged JCE. Here again, all questions of inference and weight of evidence are swept away in favor of general conclusions that go far beyond the evidence adduced in the sections of the Judgment referenced in the footnotes.

For example, Paragraph 964 states that he attended Standing Committee and other meetings at which the common purpose "to implement rapid socialist revolution and defend the country, as well as the policies necessary to achieve the common purpose, were planned and decided upon." The next seven paragraphs continue with general statements that he attended meetings where Khmer Rouge policies were decided upon. The only references in these sections are to previous sections of the Judgment where, as it was seen, it was admitted that Khieu Samphan only attended some Standing Committee and other meetings, and where there was virtually no evidence that proved why he was there, what his role was, or whether he participated in any way in the decisions taken. The theory of monolithic decision-making is used by the Chamber to attempt to make up for these evidentiary gaps, and here, in this section establishing his role in the JCE, those evidentiary gaps are nowhere discussed, nor is the theory of monolithic decision-making referenced and elaborated. We may recall, however, the Chamber's own contradiction of its finding concerning the central importance of "democratic centralism" in collective decision-making: "the Chamber is unable to conclude that unanimity was required in decision-making, and therefore leaves open the possibility that individual members may have disagreed with particular decisions from time to time."[378]

Relying nonetheless on the inferences to be drawn from Khieu Samphan's presence at meetings, and on the basis of these eight paragraphs of conclusory statements, which are devoid of any analysis and do not weigh the evidence or consider the Defense arguments as to the meetings and policies mentioned, the Chamber concludes that it is, "therefore satisfied that his attendance at meetings and contributions to plans of the Party Centre demonstrate that he not only shared the common purpose … but that he also played a key role in formulating the content of the common purpose and policies."[379] How "attendance" is transformed into a "key role" in policy formulation remains unstated. These, and other such conclusions in this section of the Judgment, do not reference the standard of proof or indicate how the Chamber arrived at these conclusions beyond a reasonable doubt. Based on the evidence cited, but seldom analyzed or weighed, in the preceding sections of the Judgment, it is difficult to see how the Chamber arrives at the conclusion that Khieu Samphan's attendance at meetings establishes that he shared the common purpose of the alleged JCE. It is even more difficult to understand how the Chamber reaches the further conclusion that he "played a key role" in determining these policies and purposes, in direct contradiction with the expert opinion of witness Philip Short, whose assessment the Tribunal otherwise held in very high esteem.[380]

In Section 16.2.2, "Intent," the Judgment turns explicitly to its final conclusion as to the required element of intent in regard to Khieu Samphan's participation in the JCE. This crucial element is established to the Chamber's satisfaction in three short paragraphs.[381] The first merely states that his continuing participation in the JCE "indicates his criminal intent." The next two paragraphs purport to support this conclusion merely by stating that "he participated in meetings, congresses, and conferences where the common purpose" and the policies to implement it were developed. In the next sentence the Judgment states, in keeping with the strategy referenced above, that Khieu Samphan "knew of the substantial likelihood that crimes would result from the implementation of these policies." The final paragraph concludes that because he knew of the substantial likelihood that the crimes might be committed, and because he was aware that they were being committed, he shared the common purpose of the JCE and intended to bring about the common purpose through the implementation of policies that involved the commission of crimes.[382]

As already addressed previously in this report, awareness of a likelihood that crimes may be committed in the future does not establish the intent required for JCE I. That shared intent is a prerequisite to a finding of JCE I, and a precondition to JCE III, which itself is not a theory of liability within the purview of the Chamber. The Chamber's conclusions about "substantial likelihood" thus cannot support its finding that Khieu Samphan possessed the required intent. Neither can the fact that he was generally aware that crimes were being committed support the conclusion that he shared the criminal intent of the members of the alleged JCE. As the *Krstic* Appeals Judgment at the ICTY made clear, awareness of the criminal intent of members of a JCE and the provision of material support to the implementation of the JCE can only establish that the Accused aided and abetted the JCE, not that he had the intent to further a shared common purpose. It was on this basis that the Appeals Chamber reversed the conviction of *Krstic* and substituted a verdict of aiding and abetting a JCE to commit genocide at Srebrenica. Thus, although the Chamber previously correctly set out the required elements of JCE I, it did not apply the legal standard correctly. The conclusions about JCE in regard to Khieu Samphan are thus legally flawed, and also are not supported by a reasoned analysis of the available evidence demonstrating the required factual basis beyond a reasonable doubt.

Part IV: Conclusion

While the Judgment rendered by the Trial Chamber on 7 August 2014 in Case 002/01 marked an important milestone in the proceedings at the ECCC, flaws in the trial process and the final Judgment overshadow the verdicts against the two Khmer Rouge leaders. While the massive scope of the Closing Order in Case 002 presented significant challenges in regard to trial management and the potential duration of the proceedings, the severance strategy adopted by the Trial Chamber was not successful in meeting those challenges. Indeed, severance of Case 002/01 had negative procedural and substantive repercussions, the effects of which are still being felt. The severance of Case 002/01 resulted in protracted uncertainty and created new trial management challenges that added significantly to the duration and complexity of the trial, rather than expediting it. The Parties challenged the validity of the Severance Order throughout the trial, and the Supreme Court Chamber eventually annulled the Order a year and a half into the proceedings. However, as detailed above, this ruling did not ultimately resolve any of the issues, because the Trial Chamber elected to subsequently re-sever the case in almost exactly the same way and continue the proceedings. The Supreme Court Chamber had acknowledged the serious impact of leaving the scope of the charges unclear throughout the trial, but in the end nothing was done to address the consequences this had on Case 002/01. The decision of the Supreme Chamber to let the renewed severance stand indicates that pragmatism may have superseded concerns of justice and fairness in the proceedings.

Another cause of procedural controversy in the trial proceedings were the repeated concerns expressed at trial over the treatment of documentary evidence by the Trial Chamber, including the limitations the Chamber's procedural decisions placed on the right of confrontation in the name of expediency. For example, the Trial Chamber decided to admit a large body of prior statements into evidence without calling these witnesses to testify in Court, thus leaving this evidence largely untested. The Trial Chamber justified its decision, against Defense objections, with reference to expediency, and by saying that such testimony would not bear upon the alleged criminal conduct of the Accused as set out in the Closing Order. Our analysis of the Judgment, however, indicates that the Chamber did in fact rely repeatedly upon such statements to establish the administrative and communications structures of the Khmer Rouge. It then used these findings to infer the *de facto* control of the Accused over direct perpetrators of crimes, and this in turn formed the basis for convictions of the Accused under Joint Criminal Enterprise and Superior Responsibility theories. The Chamber reached these findings without any reference to corroborating evidence specific to the alleged criminal acts of the Accused. This manner of proceeding would thus appear to have denied the Accused meaningful rights of confrontation. It remains to be seen whether the Supreme Court Chamber will validate the Trial Chamber's prioritization of the right to an expeditious trial over other fair trial rights of the Accused.

The general response to all the Defense concerns on documentary evidence was a promise, repeated through the documentary hearing decisions and articulated again in the Judgment, that of course the Chamber would undertake a careful assessment of probative value of any evidence relied upon in the end.

The Trial Chamber promised that it would consider all irregularities in witnesses' interviews from the investigative phase, as well as discrepancies between these interviews and the testimony witnesses gave at trial, when determining the probative value and weight to be accorded to the evidence in the Judgment. However, the rest of the Judgment contains no actual explicit consideration of any Party objections to the probative value of evidence. There is a general recitation of the factors that are relevant to analyzing the probative value of evidence, but there are literally only a handful of instances in the rest of the 630-page Judgment where the Trial Chamber actually demonstrates this weighing of various factors in order to justify reliance on a particular piece of evidence. This is true for documentary and testimonial evidence from regular witnesses, expert witnesses, and Civil Parties alike. One is left to simply presume that the Chamber conducted such an analysis, although as was discussed in Part III of this report, the quality of the factual findings and legal conclusions leave ample basis to doubt such analysis took place. To further complicate evidentiary matters, the Judgment also uses victim impact statements or statements of suffering to support its factual findings relevant to liability of the Accused, despite its previous assurances at trial that the sole purpose of the victim impact statements was to determine matters relevant to reparations and sentencing. The Chamber had assured the Defense that the statements would not be relevant to establishing the guilt of the Accused and, hence, on this basis denied the Defense an opportunity to confront consequential evidence.

The confusion of the severance, combined with a serious erosion of confrontation rights and the persistent failure of the Judgment to carefully weigh and analyze the probative value of the evidence on which the Chamber relied, give ample reason to question the soundness and legitimacy of the factual and legal findings in the Case 002/01 Judgment. A close reading of this important document only deepens the cause for concern. As discussed at length in this report, the Judgment is inadequate in its failure to meet expected standards for a final, written reasoned decision. Sound legal judgments are based on a systematic application of the elements of crimes to a well-documented body of factual findings, reached through a careful analysis of the weight and credibility of the testimony and evidence bearing on each charge in the indictment, and taking into account the competing contentions of the Defense and Prosecution on each element. Falling far below this standard, the Judgment in Case 002/01 offers a poorly organized, ill-documented, and meandering narrative in lieu of clearly structured legal writing based upon a thorough and balanced analysis of the legal and factual issues in dispute.

What distinguishes this Judgment from the standard practices of other tribunals is the lack of a coherent structure for organizing the evidence and analysis in a series of factual findings, based upon the elements in regard to each charge against the Accused. Also missing is a systematic weighing of that evidence based upon clearly articulated legal standards and a discussion of relative credibility. In the almost complete absence of such structured analysis, the basis of the factual findings scattered throughout the Judgment remain largely obscure. Narrative format operates to defeat the juristic analysis, which is the core of a well-reasoned opinion. Again and again, the Judgment draws inferences from a factual narrative that assumes rather than justifies the validity of those inferences. This is particularly apparent in the treatment of the key issue as to what inferences can reasonably be drawn from the incomplete and often contradictory evidence about the attendance or participation of the Accused in key meetings of the Khmer Rouge leadership. Proof of guilt beyond a reasonable doubt requires a solid factual foundation of findings pointing to shared intent and effective control, which are essential elements of the theories of liability employed by the Judgment. Almost entirely lacking in the Chamber's treatment of this evidence is an analysis of whether those inferences and their factual basis meet the reasonable doubt standard of proof according to the systematic application of criteria for assessing credibility and probative value.

In addition to the lack of systematic and cogent analysis for the factual findings, the application of legal doctrines to the facts also provides cause for concern throughout the Judgment. In particular, the manner in which the Judgment employs Joint Criminal Enterprise and Superior Responsibility as key theories of liability reflects incomplete research, inaccuracies, and misapprehension of significant aspects of these doctrines and the applicable jurisprudence on which they are based. While this report asserts no conclusive opinion as to the ultimate question of the liability of the Accused, the serious shortcomings of the Judgment cannot be ignored. We offer the critical assessment herein with the hope that it will provide the basis for addressing these concerns in Case 002/02 and any subsequent trials at the ECCC.

Notes

[1] Judgment, *Nuon Chea and Khieu Samphan,* (Case 00219-09-2007/ECCC/TC), Trial Chamber, 7 August 2014 (hereinafter "Case 002/01 Judgment").

[2] Ibid, at paras 1105-1107.

[3] 3,869 Civil Parties were admitted in Case 002 and formed part of the consolidated group at the commencement of trial. However, over the course of the trial, the death and withdrawal of Civil Parties from the case reduced the total number of Civil Parties still participating in the case at the time the Judgment was issued. Note that there is some discrepancy between the number of Civil Parties referenced in the Trial Chamber's Judgment and Annex I to the Judgment outlining the procedural history of the case. At paragraph three of the Judgment, the Trial Chamber incorrectly states that the Co-Investigating Judges' admitted 3,866 Civil Parties in its' Closing Order issued on 15 September 2010. Subsequently, at paragraph 1111 of the Case 002/01 Judgment, the Chamber correctly states that the Co-Investigating Judges admitted only 2,123 Civil Parties, which then increased to 3,869 following the Pre-Trial Chamber Appeals. The Procedural History annexed to the Trial Chamber's Judgment states that there were 3,867 Civil Parties at the time the Judgment was issued, however this figure is not mentioned in the Case 002/01 Judgment. See Case 002/01 Judgment, Annex I, Procedural History, at para 8; Case 002/01 Judgment, at paras 3 and 1111; and the Decision on Appeals against Orders of the Co-Investigating Judges on the Admissibility of Civil Party Applications, *Nuon Chea and Khieu Samphan, Ieng Thirith and Ieng Sary* (Case No.002/19-09-2007), Pre-Trial Chamber, 24 June 2011 and 1 July 2011.

[4] For more information, see Extraordinary Chambers in the Courts of Cambodia, "Civil Party," available at http://www.eccc.gov.kh/en/tags/topic/65 (last visited 7 September 2015).

[5] Nuon Chea's Appeal Against the Judgment in Case 002/01, (Case 002/19-09-2007-ECCC/TC), Supreme Court Chamber, 29 December 2014 (hereinafter "NC Case 002/01 Appeal"); Khieu Samphan's Appeal Against the Judgment in Case 002/01, (Case 002/19-09-2007-ECCC/TC), Supreme Court Chamber, 29 December 2014; Co-Prosecutor's Appeal Against the Judgment in Case 002/01, (Case 002/19-09-2007-ECCC/TC), Supreme Court Chamber, 28 November 2014 (hereinafter "OCP Case 002/01 Appeal").

[6] ECCC Press Release, "Swearing in of national and international judges and co-prosecutors," 3 July 2006, available online at http://www.eccc.gov.kh/en/gallery/photo/swearing-national-and-international-judges-and-co-prosecutors (last visited 7 September 2015).

[7] See *infra* Part II.C.

[8] Regarding difficulties experienced at other international criminal tribunals, see e.g., H.B. Jallow, "International Criminal Justice: Reflections on the Past and the Future," 36:2 *Commonwealth Law Bulletin* (2010), at 269-280.

[9] See Extraordinary Chambers in the Courts of Cambodia, "Civil Party," *supra* note 4.

[10] See Extraordinary Chambers in the Courts of Cambodia, "Case 001 summary," available at http://www.eccc.gov.kh/en/case/topic/1 (last visited 7 September 2015).

[11] Ibid.

[12] Judgment, *Kaing Guek Eav alias Duch,* (Case 001/18-07-2007/ECCC/TC), Trial Chamber, 26 July 2010, paras 651-657 (hereinafter Case 001 Judgment).

[13] Closing Order, *Kaing Guek Eav alias Duch* (Case 00118-07-2007/ECCC/OCIJ), Office of the Co-Investigating Judges, 8 August 2008 (hereinafter "Case 001 Closing Order").

[14] Closing Order, *Nuon Chea and Khieu Samphan, Ieng Thirith and Ieng Sary* (Case No.002/19-09-2007), Office of the Co-Investigating Judges, 15 September 2010 (hereinafter "Case 002 Closing Order").

[15] Extraordinary Chambers in the Courts of Cambodia, Internal Rules, Revision 8, 22 August 2011; Law on the Establishment of the Extraordinary Chambers, with the inclusion of amendments dated 27 October 2004 (NS/RKM/1004/006), Article 33(new) (hereinafter "ECCC Law").

[16] Note that Civil Parties at the International Criminal Court can seek individual, collective, or a combination of reparations, whereas the ECCC framework only permits collective and moral reparations. See further discussion about the difference between the Civil Party participation scheme at the Extraordinary Chambers in the Courts of Cambodia and the International Criminal Court in: Decision on Civil Party Participation in Provisional Detention Appeals, *Nuon Chea* (Case No.002/19-09-2007-ECCC/OCIJ), Pre-Trial Chamber, 20 March 2008, at para 49; B. McGonigle, "Two for the Price of One: Attempts by the Extraordinary Chambers in the Courts of Cambodia to Combine Retributive and Restorative Justice. Principles," 22 *Leiden Journal of International Law* (2009) at 142; E. Stover, M. Balthazard, and K.A. Koening, "Confronting Duch: Civil Party Participation in Case 001 at the Extraordinary Chambers in the Courts of Cambodia," 93 *International Review of the Red Cross* (2011) 882, at 11-14; and M. Mohan, "The Paradox of Victim-Centricism: Victim Participation at the Khmer Rouge Tribunal," 9 *International Criminal Law Review* (2009) 733-735, at 745-747." In relation to qualitative aspects of representation, see J.D. Ciorciari and A. Heindel, *Hybrid Justice: The Extraordinary Chambers in the Courts of Cambodia* (United States of America: The University of Michigan Press, 2014), at 203-204.

[17] At the time of publication of this report, the Internal Rules were on their ninth revision. All revised iterations of the Internal Rules are available online at http://www.eccc.gov.kh/en/document/legal/internal-rules (last accessed 7 September 2015).

[18] Amendments to the Civil Party scheme were reflected in amendments made to the Internal Rules of the Extraordinary Chambers in the Courts of Cambodia. See Extraordinary Chambers in the Courts of Cambodia, Internal Rules, first adopted on 12 June 2007; Internal Rules, Revision 1, adopted on 1 February 2008 (in force on 10 February 2008); Internal Rules, Revision 2, adopted on 5 September 2008 (in force on 15 September 2008); Internal Rules, Revision 3, adopted on 6 March 2009 (in force on 16 March 2009); Internal Rules, Revision 4, adopted on 11 September 2009 (in force on 21 September 2009); Internal Rules, Revision 5, adopted on 9 February 2010 (in force on 19 February 2010); Internal Rules, Revision 6, adopted on 17 September 2010 (in force on 27 September 2010); Internal Rules, Revision 7, adopted on 23 February 2011 (in force on 5 March 2011); Internal Rules, Revision 8, adopted on 12 August 2011 (in force on 22 August 2011); and following the Judgment in Case 002/01, Internal Rules, Revision 9, adopted on 16 January 2015 (in force on 26 January 2015). For discussion on the reasons behind the change in the Court's approach to victim participation, see B. McGonigle, *supra* note 16, at 143; G. Acquaviva, "New Paths in International Criminal Justice?" 6 *Journal of international Criminal Justice* (2008) 129 at 140-1; M. Mohan, *supra* note 16, at 754 (claiming the shift was related to the actions of Civil Party Lawyer Theary Seng during Case 001 proceedings).

[19] See *infra* Part II.B.6 for further discussion on controversy over use of Civil Party testimony in the Case 002/01 Judgment.

[20] Asian International Justice Initiative, *KRT Trial Monitor*, Issue 2, 29-31 August 2011, http://krtmonitor.org/2011/08/31/krt-trial-monitor-issue-no-2-2/ (last visited 7 September 2015).

[21] Asian International Justice Initiative, *KRT Trial Monitor*, Issue 1, 27-30 June 2011, http://krtmonitor.org/tag/krt-trial-monitor-report-issue-no-1/ (last visited 7 September 2015).

[22] See Asian International Justice Initiative, *KRT Trial Monitor,* Issue 1, 27-30 June 2011, http://krtmonitor.org/tag/krt-trial-monitor-report-issue-no-1/ (last visited 07 September 2015); Asian International Justice Initiative, *KRT Trial Monitor*, Issue 2, 29-31 August 2011, http://krtmonitor.org/2011/08/31/krt-trial-monitor-issue-no-2-2/ (last visited 7 September 2015).

[23] See Case 002/01 Judgment, *supra* note 1, at para 5: regarding the explanation of severance, the Trial Chamber stated, "in order to safeguard its ability to reach a timely judgment in Case 002 given the length and complexity of the Closing Order as well as the physical frailty and advanced age of all Accused, the Chamber issued a severance order pursuant to Internal Rule 89ter."

[24] See Order, *Nuon Chea and Khieu Samphan, Ieng Thirith and Ieng Sary*, (Case 00219-09-2007/ECCC/TC), "Severance Order pursuant to Internal Rule 89*ter*," Trial Chamber, 22 September 2011, para 2.2 (hereinafter "First Severance Decision").

[25] Forced movement of the population of Phnom Penh beginning on 17 April 1975 ("Phase One"), and the subsequent forced transfer of hundreds of thousands of Cambodians to the north of the country between late 1975 and 1977 ("Phase Two").

[26] See First Severance Decision, *supra* note 24, at "Annex: Lists of Paragraphs and Portions of the Closing Order relevant to Case 002/01, amended further to the Trial Chamber's Decision to IENG Thirith's Fitness to Stand Trial (EI38) and the Trial Chamber's Decision on the Co-Prosecutor's Request to Include Additional Crime Sites within the Scope of Trial in Case 002/01."

[27] See e.g., Cambodia Center for Human Rights, "Severance of Proceedings in Case 002 at the Extraordinary Chambers in the Courts of Cambodia," CCHR Briefing Note, October 2013, available online at http://sithi.org/tmp/admin/article/files/CCHR%20Briefing%20Note%20-%20Severance%20of%20Proceedings

%20in%20Case%20002%20at%20the%20Extraordinary%20Chambers%20in%20the%20Courts%20of%20Cambodia%20-%20October%202013%20%28ENG%29.pdf (last visited 7 September 2015).

[28] Decision, *Ieng Thirith, Ieng Sary, Nuon Chea, and Khieu Samphan* (Case 00219-9-2007/ECCC/TC), "Decision on the Co-Prosecutors Request for Reconsideration of the Terms of the Trial Chamber's Severance Order (E124/2) and the Related Motions and Annexes," Trial Chamber, 18 October 2011. See also Notice, *Ieng Thirith, Ieng Sary, Nuon Chea, and Khieu Samphan* (Case 00219-9-2007/ECCC/TC), "Notice of Trial Chamber's disposition of remaining pre-trial motions (E20, E132, E134, E135, E124/8, E124/9, E124/10, E136 and E139) and further guidance to the Civil Party Lead Co-Lawyers," Trial Chamber, 29 November 2011. See also Asian International Justice Initiative, *KRT Trial Monitor*, Issue 6, 5-9 December 2011, available at http://krtmonitor.org/2011/12/09/krt-trial-monitor-issue-no-6/ (last visited 7 September 2015).

[29] "Decision of Reassessment of Accused IENG Thirith's Fitness to Stand Trial Following Supreme Court Chamber Decision of 13 December 2011," *Ieng Thirith* (Case 00219-09-2007/ECCC/TC), Trial Chamber, 13 September 2012. See also Asian International Justice Initiative, *KRT Monitoring Special Report: Ieng Thirith's Fitness to Stand Trial*, available at https://krttrialmonitor.files.wordpress.com/2013/01/specialreport-iengthirith-final.pdf (last visited 7 September 2015).

[30] See *infra* Part II.C for further discussion.

[31] See *infra* Part II.B for further discussion.

[32] Request, *Ieng Sary, Nuon Chea and Khieu Samphan* (Case 00219-9-2007/ECCC/TC), "Co-Prosecutors' request to include additional crime sites within the scope of trial in case 002/1," Office of the Co-Prosecutors, 27 January 2012.

[33] Decision, *Ieng Sary, Nuon Chea and Khieu Samphan* (Case 00219-9-2007/ECCC/TC), "Decision on the Co-Prosecutors' Immediate Appeal of the Trial Chamber's Decision Concerning the Scope of Case 002/01," Supreme Court Chamber, 8 February 2013 (hereinafter "First SCC Decision on Severance").

[34] Decision, *Nuon Chea and Khieu Samphan* (Case 00219-9-2007/ECCC/TC), "Decision on Severance of Case 002 Following Supreme Court Chamber Decision of 8 February 2013," Trial Chamber, 26 April 2013 (hereinafter "Second Severance Decision").

[35] Decision, *Nuon Chea and Khieu Samphan* (Case 00219-9-2007/ECCC/SCC), "Decision on Immediate Appeals Against Trial Chamber's Second Decision on Severance of Case 002," Supreme Court Chamber, 25 November 2013 (hereinafter "Second SCC Decision on Severance").

[36] See Asian International Justice Initiative, *KRT Trial Monitor,* Issue 27, 19-12 June 2012, available at https://krttrialmonitor.files.wordpress.com/2012/07/27-week22-19-21june_final.pdf (last visited 7 September 2015).

[37] See Asian International Justice Initiative, *KRT Trial Monitor*, Issue 53, 18-21 February 2013; and Asian International Justice Initiative, *KRT Trial Monitor*, Issue 56, 8-12 April 2013, available at http://krtmonitor.org/2013/04/12/krt-trial-monitor-c002-issue-56-8-12-april-2013/ (visited 7 September 2015).

[38] See Asian International Justice Initiative, *KRT Trial Monitor*, Issue 39, 8-19 October 2012, available at http://krtmonitor.org/2012/10/10/krt-trial-monitor-c002-issue-39-8-10-october-2012/ (last visited 7 September 2015).

[39] See e.g., Memo, *Nuon Chea and Khieu Samphan* (Case 00219-9-2007/ECCC/TC), "Notice of Trial Chamber's disposition of remaining pre-trial motions (E20, E132, E134, E135, E124/8, E124/9, E124/10, E136 and E139) and further guidance to the Civil Party Lead Co-Lawyers," Trial Chamber, 29 November 2011; Memo, *Nuon Chea and Khieu Samphan* (Case 00219-9-2007/ECCC/TC), "Trial Chamber response to Motions E67, E57, E56, E58, E23, E59, E20, E33, E71 and E73 following Trial Management Meeting of 5 April 2011," Trial Chamber, 8 April 2011.

[40] See ECCC Law, *supra* note 15, Article 44; Memo, *Nuon Chea and Khieu Samphan* (Case 00219-9-2007/ECCC/TC), "Response to Motions E246 and E185/1/1 and other sundry requests concerning documents and deadlines," Trial Chamber, 13 February 2013.

[41] See United Nations Press Release, "Cambodia, Partners Must Address Chronic Financial Crisis Affecting Extraordinary Chambers, Deputy Secretary-General Tells Pledging Conference," 7 November 2013, available at http://www.un.org/press/en/2013/dsgsm723.doc.htm (last visited 7 September 2015).

[42] See Asian International Justice Initiative, *KRT Trial Monitor*, Issue 41, 22-25 October 2012, available at http://krtmonitor.org/2012/10/25/krt-trial-monitor-c002-issue-41-22-25-october-2012/ (last visited 7 September 2015).

[43] L. Crothers, "KR Tribunal Stopped by Strike Over Salaries," *The Cambodian Daily*, 6 March 2013, available at *The Cambodia Daily https://www.cambodiadaily.com/archives/kr-tribunal-stopped-by-strike-over-salaries-12505/ (visited 7 September 2015).* See also Asian International Justice Initiative, *KRT Trial Monitor*, Issue 54, 4 March 2013, available at (visited 7 September 2015).

[44] ECCC, "Donations Redirected to Fund National Staff Salaries as a Temporary Solution," 59 *The Court Report*, April 2013, available at http://www.eccc.gov.kh/sites/default/files/publications/April%202013%20Court%20Report _FINAL.pdf (last visited 7 September 2015).

[45] See ECCC, "Information regarding absent national staff members," 3 September 2014, available at http://www.eccc.gov.kh/en/articles/information-regarding-absent-national-staff-members (last visited 7 September 2015).

[46] *Supra,* note 41.

[47] Ibid.

[48] Extraordinary Chambers in the Courts of Cambodia, "Case 002/01 Summary of Judgment," 7 August 2014, available at http://www.eccc.gov.kh/en/tags/topic/65 (last visited 7 September 2015).

[49] See *infra* Part II.B for discussion of controversy.

[50] See "Case 002/01 Summary of Judgment," *supra* note 48.

[51] Ibid.

[52] Readers interested in a more detailed account can refer to the *KRT Trial Monitor* weekly reports from the trial, available at http://krtmonitor.org/ (last visited 7 September 2015).

[53] Asian International Justice Initiative, *KRT Trial Monitor*, Issue 6, 5-9 December 2011, available at http://krtmonitor.org/2011/12/09/krt-trial-monitor-issue-no-6/ (last visited 7 September 2015).

[54] See e.g., Asian International Justice Initiative, *KRT Trial Monitor*, Issue 6, Issue 10, Issue 37, Issue 48, and Issue 66, available at http://krtmonitor.org/category/reports-2/case-002-reports/case-00201-case-002-reports/ (last visited 7 September 2015).

[55] See Asian International Justice Initiative, *KRT Trial Monitor*, Issue 46, 11-14 December 2012, available at http://krtmonitor.org/2012/12/14/krt-trial-monitor-c002-issue-46-11-14-december-2012/ (last visited 7 September 2015).

[56] See Asian International Justice Initiative, *KRT Trial Monitor*, Issue 57, 22-27 April 2013, available at http://krtmonitor.org/2013/04/27/krt-trial-monitor-c002-issue-57-22-27-april-2013/ (last visited 7 September 2015).

[57] See Asian International Justice Initiative, *KRT Trial Monitor*, Issue 65, 24-27 June 2013, available at http://krtmonitor.org/2013/06/27/krt-trial-monitor-c002-issue-65-24-27-june-2013/ (last visited 7 September 2015).

[58] See e.g., Request, *Ieng Thirith, Ieng Sary, Nuon Chea, and Khieu Samphan* (Case 00219-9-2007/ECCC/TC), "Request for Reconsideration of Severance Order Pursuant to Internal Rule 89ter," Office of the Co-Prosecutors, 3 October 2011.

[59] Ibid.

[60] Ibid, at paras 3 and 36.

[61] Ibid, the OCP had sought to include Phase One but exclude Phase Two population movements, and to add nine specific crime sites to the scope of the inquiry: the District 12 and Tuol Po Chrey execution sites; the S-21 security center (including the purges of cadres from the "New North," Central "Old North," and East Zones sent to S-21, but excluding the Prey Sar worksite); the North Zone, Kraing Ta Chan, and Au Kanseng security centers; the Kampong Chhnang Airport construction site; and the Tram Kok cooperatives.

[62] "Request to Include Additional Crime Sites within the Scope of Trial in Case 002/01," *Ieng Sary, Nuon Chea and Khieu Samphan* (Case 00219-9-2007/ECCC/TC), Office of the Co-Prosecutors, 27 January 2012, paras 4 and 33, referring to connected paragraphs of the Case 002 Closing Order, *supra* note 14.

[63] See reference to oral arguments raised by the Parties during court relevant to the severance in Asian International Justice Initiative, *KRT Trial Monitor*, Issues 12-40, available at http://krtmonitor.org/category/reports-2/case-002-reports/case-00201-case-002-reports/ (last visited 7 September 2015).

[64] Ibid.

[65] Ibid.

[66] Memorandum, *Ieng Sary, Nuon Chea and Khieu Samphan* (Case 00219-9-2007/ECCC/TC)," Notification of Decision on Co-Prosecutors' Request to Include Additional Crime Sites within the Scope of Trial in Case 002/01 (E163) and deadline for submission of applicable law portion of Closing Briefs," Trial Chamber, 8 October 2012, para 3.

[67] Memorandum, *Ieng Sary, Nuon Chea and Khieu Samphan* (Case 00219-9-2007/ECCC/TC)," Notification of Decision on Co-Prosecutors' Request to Include Additional Crime Sites within the Scope of Trial in Case 002/01 (E163) and deadline for submission of applicable law potion of Closing Briefs," Trial Chamber, 8 October 2012, para 3.

[68] Appeal, *Ieng Sary, Nuon Chea and Khieu Samphan* (Case 00219-9-2007/ECCC/TC), "Co-Prosecutors' Immediate Appeal of Decision Concerning the Scope of Trial in Case 002/01 with Annex I and Confidential Annex II," Office of the Co-Prosecutors, 7 November 2012.

[69] See First SCC Decision on Severance, *supra* note 33.

[70] Ibid, at paras 41 and 48.

[71] Ibid, at para 48.

[72] Ibid, at para 46.

[73] Ibid, at paras 47 and 50.

[74] Memorandum, *Ieng Sary, Nuon Chea and Khieu Samphan* (Case 00219-9-2007/ECCC/TC), "Supplementary question to the parties following hearing 18 February 2013 in consequence of the Supreme Court Chamber's Decision on Co-Prosecutors Immediate Appeal of the Trial Chamber's Decision regarding the Scope," Trial Chamber, para. 8. (doc. Number of this doc is E264) E284(without, which the original cite said…/8/4) is a decision by the TC titled "Decision on Severance of Case 002/01 following Supreme Court Chamber Decision of 8 February 2013," 26 April 2013; See Asian International Justice Initiative, *KRT Trial Monitor*, Issue 53, 18-21 February 2013, available at http://krtmonitor.org/2013/02/21/krt-trial-monitor-c002-issue-53-18-21-february-2013/ (last visited 7 September 2015).

[75] See Asian International Justice Initiative, *KRT Trial Monitor*, Issue 56, 8-12 April 2013, available at http://krtmonitor.org/2013/04/12/krt-trial-monitor-c002-issue-56-8-12-april-2013/ (last visited 7 September 2015).

[76] Trial Chamber, Transcript of Trial Day 163 (29 March 2013), Case No. 002/19-09-2007, E1/176.1, lines 13-17, page 4.

[77] See Asian International Justice Initiative, *KRT Trial Monitor*, Issue 56, 8-12 April 2013, available at http://krtmonitor.org/2013/04/12/krt-trial-monitor-c002-issue-56-8-12-april-2013/ (last visited 7 September 2015).

[78] See Second Severance Decision, *supra* note 34.

[79] See Appeal, *Nuon Chea and Khieu Samphan* (Case 00219-9-2007/ECCC/TC), "Co-prosecutors' Immediate Appeal of Second Decision on Severance," Office of the Co-Prosecutors severance, 10 May 2013, paras 3, 15-79; Appeal, *Nuon Chea and Khieu Samphan* (Case 00219-9-2007/ECCC/TC), "Immediate Appeal Against the Trial Chamber's Second Decision on Severance and Response to Co-Prosecutors Second Severance Appeal," Defense for Nuon Chea, 27 May 2013, paras 7-83.

[80] Appeal, *Nuon Chea and Khieu Samphan* (Case 00219-9-2007/ECCC/TC), "Immediate Appeal Against the Trial Chamber's Second Decision on Severance and Response to Co-Prosecutors Second Severance Appeal," Defense for Nuon Chea, 27 May 2013, para 84.

[81] See Asian International Justice Initiative, *KRT Trial Monitor*, Issue 69, 23 July 2013, available at http://krtmonitor.org/2013/09/20/krt-trial-monitor-c002-issue-69-23-july-2013-2/ (last visited 7 September 2015).

[82] Decision, *Nuon Chea and Khieu Samphan* (Case 00219-9-2007/ECCC/TC), "Decision on Immediate Appeals against Trial Chamber's Second Decision on Severance of Case 002, Summary of Reasons," Supreme Court Chamber, 23 July 2013, para 9.

[83] See Second Severance Decision, *supra* note 34.

[84] Decision, *Nuon Chea and Khieu Samphan* (Case 00219-9-2007/ECCC/TC), "Decision on Immediate Appeals against Trial Chamber's Second Decision on Severance of Case 002," Summary of Reasons, Supreme Court Chamber, 23 July 2013, at para 10.

[85] Ibid, at para 11.

[86] Ibid, at para 18.

[87] Appeal, *Nuon Chea and Khieu Samphan* (Case 00219-9-2007/ECCC/TC), "Immediate Appeal Against the Trial Chamber's Second Decision on Severance and Response to Co-Prosecutors Second Severance Appeal," Defense for Nuon Chea, 27 May 2013, para 9.

[88] Second SCC Decision on Severance, *supra* note 35, at para 11.

[89] Decision, Case *Prosecutor v. Mladic* (Case IT-09-29-T), "Decision on Consolidated Prosecution Motion to Sever the Indictment, to Conduct Separate Trials, and the Amend the Indictment," Trial Chamber, 13 October 2011, at para 31. The ICTY's Trial Chamber in *Mladic* denied a request for severance in part on the basis of this reasoning: "The Chamber considers that participating in the pre-trial preparations of one case while simultaneously participating in the judgement or appeal stage of the first trial could unfairly overburden the Accused and limit his ability to participate effectively in either. The Chamber considers that the division of time and attention that would be required of the Accused to participate in his defence to both cases could render his participation less effective and also necessitate a slower pace of proceedings for both trials. Finally, the Chamber considers that the practical considerations of two trials, such as a need to potentially retain and coordinate between two Defence teams, would also complicate the Accused's ability to participate in the preparation of his defence in each trial and further slow the severed trial proceedings."

[90] See Asian International Justice Initiative, *KRT Monitor Special Report*, "Defense Teams' Boycott," 31 October 2014, available at http://krtmonitor.org/2014/10/31/krt-trial-monitor-c00202-special-report-defense-teams-boycott-31-october-2014/ (last visited 7 September 2015).

[91] Memorandum, *Nuon Chea and Khieu Samphan* (Case 00219-9-2007/ECCC/TC), "Clarification on the Consequences of the Severance in Case 002," Trial Chamber, 13 October 2014.

[92] See sources cited in footnotes 4-11 in Decision, *Nuon Chea and Khieu Samphan* (Case 00219-9-2007/ECCC/TC), "Decision on Khieu Samphan's Immediate Appeal Against the Trial Chamber's Decision on Additional Severance of Case 002 and Scope of Case 002/02," Supreme Court Chamber, 29 July 2014.

[93] Extraordinary Chambers in the Courts of Cambodia, Internal Rule 87(3), Revision 8.

[94] Extraordinary Chambers in the Courts of Cambodia, Internal Rule 83(3), Revision 3 did not provide for appropriate identification in court as a means of putting documents before the Chamber. It reads: "... Evidence from the case file is considered put before the Chamber if its content has been summarised or read out in court."

[95] See M. Kelsall, K. Baleva, A. Nababan et al., *Lessons Learned from the Duch Trial: A Comprehensive Review of the First Case Before the ECCC* (Phnom Penh: The Asian International Justice Initiative, 2009) at 23 summarizing *KRT Monitor Report* Issue 6, Issue 9, and Issue 16.

[96] See Case 002/01 Judgment *supra* note 1, at para 23.

[97] Closing Submissions, *Nuon Chea and Khieu Samphan* (Case 00219-9-2007/ECCC/TC), "Nuon Chea's Closing Submissions in Case 002/01," Defense of Nuon Chea, 26 September 2013, para 29; citing: Document No. A110, "IENG Sary's Lawyers' Letter," 20 December 2007; Document No. A110 /I, OCIJ's Letter entitled "Response to Your Letter Dated 20 December 2007 Concerning the Conduct of the Judicial Investigation," 10 January 2008; See e.g., French Code de Procedure Penale, Arts 120, 82.1; Document No. D367, "Order Issuing Warnings under Rule 38," 25 February 2010; Document No. D367/1/S, "Decision on Appeal against the Co-Investigating Judges' Order Issuing Warnings under Rule 38," 7 June 2010; Document No. D171/S, Memorandum from Co-Investigating Judges entitled "Your 'Request for Investigative Action,' Concerning, *inter alia*, the Strategy of the Co-Investigating Judges in regard to the Judicial Investigation," 11 December 2009.

[98] Memorandum, "Response to your letter dated 20 December 2007 concerning the conduct of the judicial investigation," Trial Chamber, 10 January 2008, at page 2.

[99] See Decision, *Nuon Chea and Khieu Samphan* (Case 00219-9-2007/ECCC/TC), "Decision on Objections to Documents Proposed to be put before the Chamber on the Co-Prosecutor's Annexes A1-A5 and to Documents cited in Paragraphs of the Closing Order to the first two trial segments of Case 002/01," Trial Chamber, 9 April 2012, paras 20, 28 (hereinafter "Decision on Objections to Documents Proposed").

[100] Trial Chamber Transcript of Trial Day 22 (26 January 2012), Case No. 002/19-09-2007, E1/34.1, pages 86-87. See also Memorandum, *Case Ieng Sary, Nuon Chea and Khieu Samphan* (Case 00219-9-2007/ECCC/TC), "Trial Chamber response to portions of E 114, EII411, E131/1/9, E131/6, EI36 and EI58, E162," ("Summary of Oral Decision"), Trial Chamber, 31 January 2012, para 3.

[101] See Decision on Objections to Documents Proposed, *supra* note 99, at para 28.

[102] Ibid.

[103] Ibid, at para 28.

[104] NC Case 002/01 Appeal, *supra* note 5, para 37, footnote 82.

[105] Ibid.

[106] See Decision on Objections to Documents Proposed, *supra* note 99.

[107] Trial Chamber Transcript of Trial Day 25 (1 February 2012), Case No. 002/19-09-2007, E1/37.1, lines 13-14, page 35.

[108] Trial Chamber Transcript of Trial Day 25 (1 February 2012), Case No. 002/19-09-2007, E1/37.1, pages 36-37.

[109] See Case 002/01 Judgment, *supra* note 1, at para 158, citing "(E299.1) List of Statements Put Before Chamber."

[110] Decision, *Case Ieng Sary, Nuon Chea and Khieu Samphan* (Case 00219-9-2007), "Decision on Co-Prosecutors' rule 92 submission regarding the admission of witness statements and other documents before the Trial Chamber," Trial Chamber, 20 June 2012, para 18.

[111] Response, *Nuon Chea and Khieu Samphan* (Case No. 002/19-09-2007), "Co-Prosecutors' Response to Case 002/01 Appeals," Co-Prosecutors, 24 April 2015, at para 78.

[112] Case 002/01 Judgment, *supra* note 1, at para 31, citing Decision, *Ieng Sary, Khieu Samphan, Nuon Chea* (Case No. 002/19-09-2007), "Decision on Co-Prosecutors' rule 92 submission regarding the admission of witness statements and other documents before the Trial Chamber," Trial Chamber, 20 June 2012, at paras 21-22, 32-33, and Decision, *Nuon Chea and Khieu Samphan* (Case No. 002/19-09-2007), "Decision on Objections to the Admissibility of Witness, Victim and Civil Party Statements and Case 001 Transcripts Proposed by the Co-Prosecutors and Civil Party Lead Co-Lawyers," Trial Chamber, 5 August 2013, at paras 29-30.

[113] Case 002/01 Judgment, *supra* note 1, at para 61.

[114] See *infra* Part III for further discussion.

[115] Motions for clarification raised by the Parties during hearings revealed fundamental questions, including whether this sort of witness confrontation was allowed, and if it was, under which circumstances to confront persons who testified with documents authored by others or statements made by others. The rulings on this matter seemed not to be standardized and remained at the sole discretion of the Chamber. For a few examples when this occurred, see Asian International Justice Initiative, *KRT Trial Monitor*, Issue 6, Issue 15, Issue 16, Issue 17, and Issue 18, available at http://krtmonitor.org/category/reports-2/case-002-reports/case-00201-case-002-reports/ (last visited 7 September 2015).

[116] Order, *Nuon Chea, Ieng Sary, Ieng Thirith, Khieu Samphan* (Case No. 002/19-09-2007), "Order to File Material in Preparation for Trial," Trial Chamber, 17 January 2011, at para 12.

[117] Cambodian Criminal Procedure Code (as adopted Aug. 10, 2007), Articles 321 and 334.

[118] See e.g., Memorandum, *Nuon Chea and Khieu Samphan* (Case 00219-9-2007/ECCC/TC), "Response to the Internal Rule 87(4) requests of the Co-Prosecutors, Nuon Chea and Khieu Samphan (E236/4/1, E265, E271, E276, E276/1)," Trial Chamber, 10 April 2013, at para 2.

[119] Case 002/01 Judgment, *supra* note 1, citing "Decision Concerning New Documents and Other Related Issues," 30 April 2012, at paras 17, 23, 28, and 38.

[120] Agreement between the UN and the Royal Government of Cambodia concerning the Prosecution under Cambodian Law of Crimes committed during the period of Democratic Kampuchea (2003), Article 12(2) (hereinafter "ECCC Agreement").

[121] See ECCC Law, *supra* note 15, at Article 20(new), 23(new), 33(new); and ECCC Agreement, *supra* note 120, Art. 12(1).

[122] Decision, *Nuon Chea and Khieu Samphan* (Case No. 002/19-09-2007), "Decision on NUON Chea request to admit new documents, to initiate an investigation and to summons Mr. Rob LEMKIN," Trial Chamber, 24 July 2013, at para 20.

[123] Ibid, at para 24.

[124] Extraordinary Chambers in the Courts of Cambodia, Internal Rule 84(1).

[125] Decision, *Ieng Sary, Khieu Samphan, Nuon Chea* (Case No. 002/19-09-2007), "Decision on Co-Prosecutors' rule 92 submission regarding the admission of witness statements and other documents before the Trial Chamber," Trial Chamber, 20 June 2012, at para 18.

[126] Submission, *Nuon Chea and Khieu Samphan*, (Case No. 002/19-09-2007), "Nuon Chea's Closing Submissions in Case 002/01," Nuon Chea Defense Team, 26 September 2013, 50; "Decision on NUON Chea request to admit new documents, to initiate an investigation and to summons Mr. Rob LEMKIN," *supra* note 122, at para 24.

[127] Response, *Nuon Chea and Khieu Samphan*, (Case No. 002/19-09-2007), "Co-Prosecutors' Response to Case 002/01 Appeals," Co-Prosecutors to the Supreme Court Chamber, 24 April 2015, pages 23-26, 34-35.

[128] Response, *Nuon Chea and Khieu Samphan*, (Case No. 002/19-09-2007), "Co-Prosecutors' Response to Case 002/01 Appeals," Co-Prosecutors to Supreme Court Chamber, 24 April 2015, at para 65.

[129] See E251 "TC Decision on Defence Requests Concerning Irregularities Alleged to have Occurred during the Judicial Investigation" (E221, E223, E224, E224/2, E234, E234/2 and E241/1), 7 December 2012 ("Decision on Alleged Irregularities"), para 26.

[130] Case 002/01 Judgment, *supra* note 1, at para 34.

[131] Factors cited include: "the criteria set out in Internal Rule 87(3), the circumstances surrounding the creation or recording of evidence, whether the original or a copy was admitted, legibility, discrepancies with other versions, deficiencies credibly alleged, whether the parties had the opportunity to challenge the evidence and other indicia of reliability including chain of custody and provenance." The Chamber also claims to consider "the identification, examination, bias, source and motive—or lack thereof—of the authors and sources of the evidence." See Case 002/01 Judgment, *supra* note 1, at para 34.

[132] See *infra* at Part III for detailed discussion of missing credibility analysis.

[133] Case 002/01 Judgment, *supra* note 1, at para 66. This statement ends with a footnote directing the reader back to "Section 2: Preliminary Issues, 2.3.3 and 2.3.4 (on impartiality of the Trial Chamber and facilities and time available for the preparation of a defence.)" There is confusion arising out of an error in the reference here. Discussion of the impartiality of the Trial Chamber and facilities and time available for the preparation of a defense, in fact, appear in Sections 2.4.3 and 2.4.4, respectively. It is not clear what relevance these two sections have to demonstrating how and when "The Chamber considers these submissions and objections [pertaining to probative value of evidence] in its final assessment of the evidence." Sections 2.3.3 and 2.3.4 offer four short paragraphs explaining access to the Case File and outlining the general framework for the rules of admissibility of evidence at the ECCC, but again, none of these paragraphs contains an example of the Chamber actually taking a single submission or objection about the probative value of evidence into consideration and articulating how the Court ultimately chose to assess the weight of the evidence.

[134] Case 002/01 Judgment, *supra* note 1, at para 93, footnote 155.

[135] Ibid, at footnote 1210.

[136] Ibid, at paras 1094-1103. The Trial Chamber's consideration of potentially mitigating factors for sentencing contain six uses of the word "weight" to declare, for example, "the Chamber accords it little weight as a mitigating factor."

[137] Ibid, at para 785, footnote 2544, citing evidence of Khieu Samphan's apparent weight during the DK era (as in, how well-fed he was).

[138] Ibid, at para 14: "the overwhelming weight of the evidence" indicating that the Accused were Khmer Rouge officials between 1975 and 1979.

[139] Ibid, at para 34: reciting the general procedural approach that "Absent the opportunity to examine the source or author of evidence, less weight may be assigned to that evidence."

[140] Ibid, at para 66: stating that, "the parties availed themselves of these opportunities to make detailed submissions on matters relevant to probative value and thus weight to be assigned to evidence at the conclusion of proceedings. The Chamber considers these submissions and objections in its final assessment of the evidence."

[141] Ibid, at para 146 and 373, and footnotes 425 and 1136.

[142] Ibid, at para 31 (regarding general evidentiary and procedural principles), 59 and 61 (noting and responding to the Defense complaint that they had inadequate opportunity to challenge the credibility of witnesses testifying in Court), and para 1157 (regarding a reparations project).

[143] Ibid, at paras 80, 266, and 677.

[144] Ibid, at para 80: finding a transcript of a 1998 interview given by Nuon Chea to Khem Ngun reliable as an evidentiary basis for broad factual findings in 3.1 "General Overview and Establishment of the CPK."

[145] Ibid, at para 107: finding a would-be exculpatory aspect of witness Phy Phoun's testimony not reliable on the grounds that it was speculative and contrary to claims made by three books in evidence. The three books cited at footnote 297 are: (1) Philip Short, *Pol Pot: The History of a Nightmare*, (2) Ke Pauk, *Autobiography of Ke Pauk from 1949-1985*, and (3) W. Shawcross, *Sideshow: Kissinger, Nixon and the Destruction of Cambodia*. See also para 124 (end of FN 359) regarding the testimony of Ny Khan which, if true, would also cast doubt on whether Oudong had ever been evacuated. The Trial Chamber found the witness testimony internally inconsistent and therefore not reliable, "on the subject of the 1974 evacuation of Oudong." See also para 139, where the Chamber finds So Socheat's evidence unreliable (partly because she is Khieu Samphan's wife).

[146] Ibid, at para 667: Positively assessing the oral testimony of witness Sum Alat.

[147] Ibid, at paras 26, 36, and 621: especially regarding the description of what populations the Khmer Rouge generally deemed reliable or not, stating "Middle peasants and the petty bourgeoisie, who were deemed less reliable, were to be assigned, under the leadership of the proletariat or party members originating from the base class, to tasks secondary to farming the most fertile land."

[148] Civil Parties Closing Brief to Case 002/01 with Confidential Annexes 1-4, *Nuon Chea and Khieu Samphan,* (Case 002/19-09-2007-ECCC/TC), Trial Chamber, 26 September 2013, paras 7-8 (hereinafter "CP Closing Brief").

[149] ECCC documents issued by the Public Affairs Section have consistently referenced notions of truth, justice, and national reconciliation associated with the establishment of the Court. See *An Introduction to the Khmer Rouge Trials,* (1st to 5th Edition: Secretariat of the Royal Government Task Force, Office of the Council of Ministers, Kingdom of Cambodia, 2004-2008); B. McGonigle, *supra* note 16, at 129; J. Herman, *Local Voices in Internationalised Justice: The Experience of Civil Parties at the Extraordinary Chambers in the Courts of Cambodia,* Centre on Human Rights in Conflict, (May 2014) at 4.

[150] See generally, CP Closing Brief, *supra* note 149.

[151] See Judgment, *supra* note 1.

[152] See Case 001 Judgment, *supra* note 12.

[153] Case 002/01 Judgment, *supra* note 2.

[154] Case 001 Judgment, *supra* note 12.

[155] Calculations in table 1 include all citations to Civil Party and Witness evidence used to support factual findings in the Judgment, but excludes character witnesses. See further analysis in NC Case 002/01 Appeal, *supra* note 5.

[156] Asian International Justice Initiative, *KRT Trial Monitor,* Issue 6, 5-9 December 2011, available online at http://krtmonitor.org/2011/12/09/krt-trial-monitor-issue-no-6/ (last visited 11 March 2015); Asian International Justice Initiative, *KRT Trial Monitor,* Issue 8, 10-12 January 2012, available online at http://krtmonitor.org/2012/01/12/krt-trial-monitor-issue-no-8/ (last visited 11 March 2015).

[157] CP Closing Brief, *supra* note 149, at paras 7-8.

[158] Decision on Request to Recall Civil Party TCCP-187, for Review of Procedure Concerning Civil Parties' Statements on Suffering and Related Motions and Responses, *Nuon Chea and Khieu Samphan,* (Case 002/19-09-2007-ECCC/TC), Trial Chamber, 2 May 2013, at para 22.

[159] Decision on Request to Recall Civil Party TCCP-187, for Review of Procedure Concerning Civil Parties' Statements on Suffering and Related Motions and Responses, *Nuon Chea and Khieu Samphan,* (Case 002/19-09-2007-ECCC/TC), Trial Chamber, 2 May 2013.

[160] See Case 002/01 Judgment, *supra* note 1, at paras 14, 34, 66, 397, 502, 1094, and 1103.

[161] See discussion of credibility of witness Phy Phuon in Case 002/01 Judgment, *supra* note 1, at para 146 in footnote 425.

[162] Steve Heder refused to be called as an Expert and was ultimately summonsed as a fact witness. See Case 002/01 Judgment, *supra* note 1, at para 397.

[163] See Case 002/01 Judgment, *supra* note 1, at para 665.

[164] See e.g., Case 001 Judgment, *supra* note 12 at paras 250, 323, 484, and 485.

[165] See especially, Civil Parties Aun Phally, Sou Sotheavy, and Chheng Eng Ly, who only provided victim impact statements, not factual testimony, but whose statements were cited in the Judgment in support of factual findings. See Judgment, *Nuon Chea and Khieu Samphan, supra* note 2 at para 474; and see further discussion in NC Case 002/01 Appeal, *supra* note 5.

[166] The drafting committee comprised of You Bunleng, Mong Monichariya, Prak Kim, San Kong Srim and Sin Rith (Cambodian judges), Agnieszka Klonowiecka–Milart (Poland), Marcel Lemonde (France), Claudia Fenz (Austria), and Silvia Cartwright (New Zealand). See Joint Press Statement by the Committee, "ECCC Overcomes Complexity, Adopts Internal Rules for DK Trials," *Xinhua,* 13 June 2007, available online at http://english.peopledaily.com.cn/200706/13/eng20070613_383831.html (last visited 11 March 2015).

[167] "The new scheme as adopted is intended to balance the rights of all parties, to safeguard the ability of the ECCC to achieve its mandate while maintaining Civil Party participation, and to enhance the quality of Civil Party representation." See ECCC Press Release, "7th Plenary Session Concludes," 9 February 2010, available online at http://www.eccc.gov.kh/en/articles/7th-plenary-session-eccc-concludes (last visited 11 March 2015).

[168] See generally, Khmer Rouge Trial Monitor Reports for Case 001 and Case 002 published by the Asian International Justice Initiative, available online at http://krtmonitor.org/ (last visited 11 March 2015).

[169] Other factors which arguably impacted participation include the increased number of defendants indicted in Case 002, the relative complexity and scope of charges and crime sites in the Case 002 Closing Order, the increased number of Civil Party applications and lawyers representing victims, the limited availability of resources for victim representation, the Trial Chamber's decision to sever the case and subsequent appeals, the behavior of individual Trial Chamber judges toward Civil Parties during proceedings, delays to proceedings, and translation issues. For a comprehensive discussion, see M. Guiraud, *Victim's Rights Before the Extraordinary Chambers in the Courts of Cambodia: A Mixed Record for Civil Parties*, (International Federation for Human Rights: Phnom Penh, 2011).

[170] ECCC Press Release, "5th Plenary Session of Judicial Officers Closing Press Statement," 6 March 2009, available online at http://www.eccc.gov.kh/sites/default/files/media/closing_plenary_session_EN.pdf (last visited 11 March 2015).

[171] Ambiguities in the Internal Rules and a lack of clarity on how the Court would interpret the parameters of victim participation at the pre-trial stage had already been raised by Civil Parties as early as 2008, when Theary Seng requested, "a declaratory decision on civil party participation rights before the Pre-Trial Chamber," regarding the Court's interpretation of the Internal Rules. See "Decision on Application for Reconsideration of Civil Party's Right to Address pre-Trial Chamber in Person," *Nuon Chea and Khieu Samphan, Ieng Thirith and Ieng Sary* (Case 002/19-09-2007-ECCC/OCIJ (PTC03), 28 August 2008.

[172] Extraordinary Chambers in the Courts of Cambodia, Internal Rule 23(1), Revision 3.

[173] The authors recognize that some of the uncertainty surrounding the Civil Party scheme in Case 001 was related to the fact that Case 001 was the first trial before the ECCC. This may go some way to explaining the Trial Chamber's reluctance to confine itself to an early interpretation of the rules prior to the commencement of trial. See M. Kelsall et al., *supra* note 95, at 45-6; J.D. Ciorciari and A. Heindel, *supra* note 16, at 61; E. Hoven, "Civil Party Participation in Trials of Mass Crimes: A Qualitative Study at the Extraordinary Chambers in the Courts of Cambodia," *Journal of International Criminal Justice* (2014) at 26; E. Stover, M. Balthazard, and K.A Koening, *supra* note 16, at 21-22; M. Guiraud, *Victim's Rights Before the Extraordinary Chambers in the Courts of Cambodia: A Mixed Record for Civil Parties*, (International Federation for Human Rights: Phnom Penh, 2011) at 19; A. Werner and D. Rudy, "Civil Party Representation at the ECCC: Sounding the Retreat in International Criminal Law?" 8 *Northwestern Journal of International Human Rights*, 3 (2010), 301-309, at 302.

[174] The Extraordinary Chambers in the Courts of Cambodia, "Sixth ECCC Plenary Session Concludes," 20 March 2011, available online at http://www.eccc.gov.kh/en/articles/sixth-eccc-plenary-session-concludes (last visited 11 March 2015).

[175] For consensus on the need for change even amongst Civil Party Lawyers see A. Werner and D. Rudy, *supra* note 173, at 304; M. Guiraud, *Victim's Rights Before the Extraordinary Chambers in the Courts of Cambodia: A Mixed Record for Civil Parties*, (International Federation for Human Rights: Phnom Penh, 2011) at 19-20; M. Kelsall, et al., *supra* note 95, at 37.

[176] M. Kelsall, et al., *supra* note 95, at 37.

[177] During Case 001, the OCIJ declared 28 of the 94 Civil Party applications admissible in the Closing Order. However, the admissibility of the remaining 66 applications was yet to be determined. The Internal Rules were silent on exactly when the determination on Civil Party applications was required, so the issue was left to the Trial Chamber's discretion. The procedure, unclear from a reading of the Internal Rules (Extraordinary Chambers in the Courts of Cambodia, Internal Rules, Rule 23.4 and 83.1), was a matter of contention between the Defense and the Civil Parties. Under the procedural framework in force at the time, former Rule 100.1 of the Internal Rules allowed the Trial Chamber to rule on the admissibility of Civil Party applications at any time during the proceedings.

[178] The 62 of 90 applicants that the OCIJ had not granted Civil Party status were granted interim Civil Party status by the Trial Chamber and participated as Civil Parties throughout the trial proceedings in Case 001.

[179] Asian International Justice Initiative, *KRT Trial Monitor*, Issue 19, 30 August 2009, available online at http://krtmonitor.org/2009/08/30/krt-trial-monitor-c001-issue-19-week-ending-30-august-2009/ (last visited 11 March 2015). See also discussion of the psychosocial impact of the Court's rejection of the Civil Parties in E. Stover, M. Balthazard, and K.A Koening, *supra* note 16, at 538.

[180] Since an award cannot be made against an accused person that has found to be indigent, the changes provided an additional option for the Civil Parties to seek collective and moral reparations. See Extraordinary Chambers in the Courts of Cambodia, "Eight (sic) ECCC Plenary Session Concludes," 17 September 2010, available online at http://www.eccc.gov.kh/en/articles/eight-eccc-plenary-session-concludes (last visited 15 March 2015).

[181] M. Kelsall, et al., *supra* note 95, at 32.

[182] Ibid.

[183] From Week 15 of trial proceedings in Case 001, trial monitors noted that the Civil Party groups were already required to direct their questions through one or two representatives on behalf of the entire group. See M. Kelsall, et al., *supra* note 95, at 34.

[184] Extraordinary Chambers in the Courts of Cambodia, Internal Rules, Revision 2, 15 September 2008.

[185] Extraordinary Chambers in the Courts of Cambodia, Internal Rules, Revision 8, 22 August 2011.

[186] No Civil Party Lawyers had been officially recognized at the time of the Pre-Trial Chamber Appeal Hearing concerning Duch's appeal against the provisional detention order. See Pre-Trial Chamber, Transcript of Appeal Hearing (21 November 2007), Case No. 001/18-07/2007. The first Civil Party Lawyer recognized in Case 001 was Hong Kimsuon in January 2008. See Lawyers Recognition Decision, Co-Investigating Judges, (Case 001/18-07-2007-ECCC/OCIJ), 31 January 2008. A Practice Direction on victim participation, including information on how to apply as a Civil Party, was released following the Plenary Session on 12 June 2007, during which the rules were amended to include victim participation (and entered into force on 19 June 2007). Available at: 02/2007/Rev.1 http://www.eccc.gov.kh/sites/default/files/legal-documents/PD_Victims_Participation_rev1_En.pdf (last visited 2 September 2015). See also M. Kelsall, et al., *supra* note 95, at 32 citing the Internal Rules applicable at the time (Rev.3, Rule 82.3, Rule 89 bis2).

[187] Decision, "Decision on Civil Party Participation in Provisional Detention Appeals," Pre-Trial Chamber, 20 March 2008; "Decision on Preliminary Matters Raised by the Lawyers for the Civil Parties in Ieng Sary's Appeal against Provisional Detention Order," Pre-Trial Chamber, 1 July 2008; "Directions on Civil Party Oral Submissions During the Hearing of the Appeal Against Provisional Detention Order," (Case 002/19-09-2007-ECCC/OCIJ (PTC03), Pre-Trial Chamber, 20 May 2008.

[188] Decision, *Kaing Guek Eav alias Duch*, (Case No.001/18-07-2007/ECCC/TC), "Decision on the Request of the Co-Lawyers for Civil Parties Group 2 to Make an Opening Statement during the Substantive Hearing," Trial Chamber, 27 March 2009.

[189] "Trial Chamber Response to Lead Co-Lawyers Request to make a brief Preliminary Remarks on behalf of Civil Parties," Trial Chamber Memorandum, (Case 002), 15 November 2011; "Decision on Civil Party Lead Co-Lawyers Request to Make Opening Remarks," (Case 002), Trial Chamber, 4 October 2014.

[190] See "Decision on Civil Party Co-Lawyers' Joint Request for a Ruling on the Standing of Civil Party Lawyers to Make Submissions on Sentencing and Directions Concerning the Questioning of the Accused, Experts and Witnesses Testifying on Character," (Case File 001/18-07-2007/ECCC/TC), Trial Chamber, 9 October 2009, para 25; and "Decision on the Appeals Filed by Lawyers for Civil Parties (Groups 2 and 3) Against the Trial Chamber's Oral Decisions of 27 August 2009," (Case No.001/18-07-2007/ECCC/SCC), Supreme Court Chamber, 24 December 2009. See also Judge Lavergne's dissent on this point in the Case 001 Judgment, *supra* note 12.

[191] The Trial Chamber's decision in Case 001 rejecting the request of the Civil Parties to make submissions on sentencing and put questions concerning the character of the Accused was appealed to the Supreme Court Chamber by two Civil Party groups in Case 001. In its decision, the Supreme Court Chamber declined to consider the appeal on the grounds that Internal Rule 104(4) limited an immediate appeal against the sentencing or character decision to an appeal against the Judgment on the merits. Changes to the Internal Rules then limited the scope of Civil Parties' appeals against the Trial Chamber Judgment to "the decision on reparations" generally and the verdict, but only where the Co-Prosecutors appealed. The amended rules also expressly prohibit appeals against the sentence. See ECCC, Internal Rules 104*bis* and 105, Revision 8; "Decision on the Appeals Filed by Lawyers for Civil Parties (Groups 2 and 3) Against the Trial Chamber's Oral Decisions of 27 August 2009," (Case No.001/18-07-2007/ECCC/SCC), Supreme Court Chamber, 24 December 2009; "Decision on Civil Party Co-Lawyers' Joint Request for a Ruling on the Standing of Civil Party Lawyers to Make Submissions on Sentencing and Directions Concerning the Questioning of the Accused, Experts and Witnesses Testifying on Character," Trial Chamber, 9 October 2009, para 25.

[192] Note that in Case 001, the Trial Chamber allowed Civil Parties to ask questions to the Accused through the President, but reminded the Accused of his right to remain silent. See Trial Chamber, "Transcript of Trial Day 61" (19 January 2009), Case No. 001/19-09-2007, E1/65.1, page 60, 11-21.

[193] During the statement of Civil Party Chau Ny in Case 002/01, the Trial Chamber did not permit Civil Parties to pose questions directly to the Accused Khieu Samphan, but required that they be directed through the President. See "Decision on request to recall civil party tccp-187, for review of procedure concerning Civil Parties' statements on suffering and related motions and Responses" (E240, E240/1, E250, E250/1, E267, E267/1 AND E267/2), (Case 002/19-09-2007-ECCC/TC), Trial Chamber, 2 May 2013.

[194] "Decision on Civil Party Co-lawyers' Joint Request for a Ruling on the Standing of Civil Party lawyers to Make Submissions on Sentencing and Directions Concerning the Questioning of the Accused, Experts and witnesses on Character," (Case No.001/18-07-2007/ECCC/TC), Trial Chamber, 12 October 2009.

[195] See discussion *supra*, footnote 190.

[196] In Case 001, two weeks were reserved to hear statements from 13 Civil Parties in relation to reparations claimed (17-21 August 2009). The hearings provided an avenue for the Civil Parties to express their suffering and explain their request reparations; however, the Trial Chamber approached the hearings differently. Although the hearings allowed the Civil Parties to express feelings regarding the sufferings, emotionally and physically, from the crimes alleged against the Accused, no clear distinction appears to have been made between a statement of suffering and factual testimony. Accordingly, the Defense was also provided an opportunity to question the Civil Party at the conclusion of his or her statement and did so on two occasions. During the hearings, two Civil Parties (Hav Sophea and So Som) were challenged by the Defense in relation to evidence supporting their Civil Party status. During the statements, Civil Parties were also repeatedly told to focus their statements on facts. See Trial Chamber, "Transcript of Trial Day 61," (19 August 2009), Case No. 001/19-09-2007, E3/1552, para 18. See also "Order Scheduling the Trial Proceedings for the Period of August to 17 September 2009," (Case No.001/18-07-2007/ECCC/TC), 13 August 2009; Asian International Justice Initiative, *KRT Trial Monitor*, Issue 18, Case 001, 23 August 2009.

[197] On 22 October 2012, following a request from the Civil Parties (initially made orally, but subsequently by written submission), the Trial Chamber made an oral decision during the hearing of Civil Party Yim Sovann TCCP-169 that until further notice, Civil Parties would be permitted to make statements pertaining to their suffering during the Democratic Kampuchea era generally. The Trial Chamber explicitly stated that the purpose of the statements was to enable the Chamber to assess the gravity of crimes and would not constitute evidence prejudicial to the Accused. See "Decision on Request to Recall Civil Party TCCP-187, for Review of Procedure Concerning Civil Parties' Statements of Suffering and Related Motions and Responses," Trial Chamber, 2 May 2013.

[198] The issue of whether Civil Parties would be able to address the court in person without a lawyer was raised by Civil Party Theary Seng prior to the commencement of trial proceedings in Case 001. See "Written Version of Oral Decision of 1 July 2008 on the Civil Party's Request to Address the Court in Person," (Case 002/19-09-2007-ECCC/OCIJ(PTC03), Pre-Trial Chamber, 3 July 2008; and "Decision on Application for Reconsideration of Civil Party's Right to Address pre-Trial Chamber in Person," (Case 002/19-09-2007-ECCC/OCIJ (PTC03), 28 August 2008.

[199] Extraordinary Chambers in the Courts of Cambodia, Internal Rule 12*ter*, Revision 8.

[200] An additional reason was related to efficiency and timing, given the resources that would be involved to bring the Civil Parties to the court on two separate occasions to give evidence on facts and/or to make a statement of suffering.

[201] These numbers are specified as the estimated number of victims as defined in the Closing Orders for each case. Presumably, the figures include those victims who died, but do not exclude indirect victims, which would substantially increase the numbers. See Case 002 Closing Order, *supra* note 14.

[202] In Case 001, the admissibility of Civil Party applications was determined by the Trial Chamber under the existing framework. Following amendments to the rules for Case 002, admissibility was determined by the Office of the Co-Investigating Judges. Closing Order Case 002, *supra* note 14, at para 12.

[203] The appeal on admissibility issues was determined by the Supreme Court Chamber in Case 001. Following the amendments, appeals on admissibility decided by the Office of the Co-Investigating Judges was heard by the Pre-Trial Chamber in Case 002. See "Decision on Appeals against Orders of the Co-Investigating Judges on the Admissibility of Civil Party Applications," *Nuon Chea and Khieu Samphan, Ieng Thirith and Ieng Sary* (Case No.002/19-09-2007), Pre-Trial Chamber, 24 June 2011.

[204] Comparison between the number of Civil Parties declared admissible and those who provided testimony during the case.

[205] Ninety-four Civil Parties applied for Civil Party status in Case 001. Following the withdrawal of three applications and the Trial Chamber's denial of status to a further application, 90 total applications were considered by the Trial Chamber. Seventy-six of those were accepted as Civil Parties, and 22 of these Civil Parties gave evidence.

[206] Case 001 Judgment, *supra* note 12, at para 251.

[207] The OCIJ found 2,123 Civil Parties admissible in Case 002. On appeal to the Pre-Trial Chamber, this number was increased to 3,869; 31 of these Civil Parties gave evidence in Case 002/01. See "Decision on Appeals against Orders of the Co-Investigating Judges on the Admissibility of Civil Party Applications," *Nuon Chea and Khieu Samphan, Ieng Thirith and Ieng Sary* (Case No.002/19-09-2007), 24 June 2011 and 1 July 2011.

[208] The inclusive approach adopted by the Pre-Trial Chamber to admissibility requirements in Case 002/01 resulted in almost all Civil Party applications being accepted. Comparatively, the Office of the Co-Investigating Judges adopted a more strict approach to the threshold for admissibility during Case 001. See criticism that the approach was overly strict in Case 001, and overly inclusive in Case 002, in J.D. Ciorciari and A. Heindel, *supra* note 16, at 62.

[209] M. Kelsall, et al., *supra* note 95 at 31.

[210] Asian International Justice Initiative, *KRT Trial Monitor*, Issue 20, 23-26 April 2012, available online at http://krtmonitor.org/2012/04/26/krt-trial-monitor-issue-no-20/ (last visited 11 March 2015).

211 See e.g., criticism from ECCC officers on the impact of the Civil Party Lawyers on trial efficiency in E. Hoven, *supra* note 173; See also, J.D. Ciorciari and A. Heindel, *supra* note 16, at 61. But, see the assessment of trial monitors on the impact of Civil Party Lawyers based on cumulative trial monitoring reports and transcripts in M. Kelsall, et al., *supra* note 95.

212 Monitors noted that in Case 001, the Duch Defense had consistently argued that it should be allocated equivalent time to the Prosecution and Civil Parties combined. This was not agreed to formally by the Trial Chamber, but considered on a case-by-case basis. See Asian International Justice Initiative, *KRT Trial Monitor*, Issue 9, 21 June 2009, available online at https://krttrialmonitor.files.wordpress.com/2012/07/aiji_eccc_case1_no9_21june09_en.pdf (last visited 11 March 2015) at 2.

213 See Extraordinary Chambers in the Courts of Cambodia, "Press Release: 7th Plenary Session of the ECCC Commences," (28 January 2009), available online at http://www.cambodiatribunal.org/assets/pdf/reports/eccc_pr28jan2010_eng.pdf (last visited 11 March 2015). See also comments from Dr. Stegmiller that the system is so changed that it should not be labeled as "Civil Party" participation anymore in I. Stegmiller, "Legal Developments in Civil Party Participation at the Extraordinary Chambers in the Courts of Cambodia," 27 *Leiden Journal of International Law*, (2014), 465-477, at 475.

214 For example, in Case 001, trial monitors noted that the Judges asked many irrelevant questions, and the Accused provided irrelevant and lengthy accounts that prolonged the proceedings. See comprehensive discussion in M. Kelsall, et al., *supra* note 95.

215 Trial monitors noted Civil Party Lawyer Ty Srinna had asked repetitive questions in week 14 of proceedings; see Asian International Justice Initiative, *KRT Trial Monitor*, Issue 19, 18-20 April 2012, available online https://krttrialmonitor.files.wordpress.com/2012/05/19-wk-14_18-20-april-2012.pdf (last visited 11 March 2015).

216 The proportion of time used by the Defense, Prosecution, and Civil Parties was calculated using the "start" and "finish" times published in the "Written Records of Proceedings" for each trial day. For each Party, the number of hours was calculated by adding the start and finish times and subtracting the recess breaks. Where there were multiple Parties presenting in one allotment, for example, "the Trial Chamber, Co-Prosecutors and Defense presented between 16:07 and 16:25 on the 16 December 2009," the distribution of time was divided evenly between the participating Parties. Where records only specified a start time for a given Party (but no finish time), the finish time was approximated based on the start time of the following Party. While these calculations are not exact, they provide an approximate calculation of time utilized by Parties before the ECCC during Case 001 and Case 002/01. The calculation includes time utilized by the Civil Parties for victim impact statements. For further information on the data set, please contact the Asian International Justice Initiative.

217 Analysis prepared using public ECCC documents and reporting from the Asian International Justice Initiative trial monitoring team.

218 The Lead Co-Lawyers were also the only lawyers to question witnesses Vanthan Dara Peou and Youk Chang in relation to document admissibility. The following witnesses were questioned by the Lead Co-Lawyers only: TCW 742 Tun Soeun, TCW 665 Sok Roeu, TCE 12 Chhim Sotheara, TCW 565 Al Rockoff, TCW 384 Leng Chhoeung, TCW 570 Ros Suy, TCW 428 Meas Voeun, TCW 504 Pean Khean, TCW 793 Chhang Youk, TCW 766 Vanthan Dar Peou.

219 Civil Party Lawyers and the Lead Co-Lawyers are represented as both having questioned the individual only where substantive questions were put to the individual during questioning, with reference to the full official ECCC transcript of trial proceedings for each day the individual was questioned. Where the Lead Co-Lawyers addressed the Court in order to introduce the Civil Party Lawyer designated to put questions to the witness, expert, or Civil Party, but did not put substantive questions to the individuals themselves, this was not counted in the figures (despite the fact that they may have been listed as having questioned the individual in the summary of proceedings in the ECCC official "Written Record of Proceedings" and/or index of the official trial transcript).

220 The Trial Chamber Witnesses ("TCW"), Trial Chamber Experts ("TCE"), and Trial Chamber Civil Parties ("TCCP") questioned by both the Lead Co-Lawyers for Civil Parties and at least one Civil Party Lawyer included the following individuals (surnames in all caps here, in keeping with the ECCC naming conventions): TCE 33 HEADER Stephen; TCW 617 SAUT Toeung; TCW 604 SAO Sarun; TCW 488 OEUN Tan; TCW 797 YUN Kim; TCW 564 ROCHOEM Ton; TCW 609 SA Siek, alias Sim; TCCP 28 EM Oeun; TCW 475 NOEM Sem; TCW 695 SUON Kanil; TCW126 CHUON Thi; TCCP 186 SAR Sarin; TCW 548 PRUM Sou; TCW 110 CHHOUK Rin, alias Sok (or Sokh); TCCP 169 YIM Sovann; TCCP 25 CHUM Sokha; TCCP 64 LAY Bony; TCW 661 SOKH Chhin; TCCP 188 TOENG SOKHA; TCW 536 PONCHAUD Francois; TCW 752 UNG Chhat; TCW 689 SUM Alat, alias CHHONG Lat; TCW 673 SO Socheat, alias Rin.

221 The witnesses and experts questioned only by the Civil Party Lawyers included: TCCP 185 KLAN Fit (or KLAN Vet); TCCP 123 ROMAM Yun, alias Khamphy; TCW 395 LONG Norin, alias Rith; TCW 542 PRAK Yut; TCE 11 CHANDLER David Porter; TCE 65 SHORT Philip; TCW 281 KAING Guek Eav, alias Duch; TCW 586 SALOTH Ban; TCW 487 NY Khan; TCW 583 SAKIM Lmut; TCW 323 KHOEM Ngorn; TCW 321 KHIEV Neou; TCW 490 ONG Thong Hoeung; TCW 694 SUONG Sikoeun; TCW 338 KIM Vun; TCW 480 NORNG Sophang; TCW 91

CHEA Say; TCW 320 KHIEV En; TCW 307 KHAM Phan, alias PHAN Van; TCW 620 SA Vi; TCW 648 SIM Hao, alias That, alias SEUM Hao; TCW 164 EK Hen, alias Chea, alias AEK Hen; TCW 100 CHHAOM Se; TCW 362 KUNG Kim; TCW 690 SUM Chea; TCCP 89 MOM Sam Oeurn; TCW 507 PECHUY Chipse; TCCP 82 MEAS Saran; TCCP 105 OR Ry; TCCP 187 CHAU Ny; TCCP 108 PECH Srey Phal; TCCP 59 KIM Vanndy; TCW 247 Hun Chhunly; TCCP 1 AFFONCO Denise; TCCP 116 PIN Yathay; TCW 253 IENG Phan; TCW 624 SCHANBERG Sydney Hillel; TCW 801 NOU Mouk (E266/3); TCW 505 PECH Chim; TCW 386 LEV Lam; TCW 389 LIM Sat; TCW 277 JULLIAN-GAUFRES Philippe; TCW 84 CHAU Sockon; TCCP 151 SOU Sotheavy; TCCP 2 AUN Phally; TCCP 156 THOUCH FENIES Phandarasar; TCCP 129 SANG Rath; TCCP 7 CHAN Sopheap; TCCP 100 NOU Hoan; TCCP 149 SOPHAN Sovany; TCCP 170 YIN Roumdoul; TCCP 117 PO Dina; TCCP 4 BAY Sophany; TCCP 145 SOEUN Sophany; TCCP 141 SENG Sivutha; TCCP 172 YOS Phal; TCCP 13 CHHENG Eng Ly; CCP 198 HUO Chantha.

222 The witnesses and experts questioned only by the Lead Co-Lawyers for Civil Parties included: TCW 742 Tun Soeun, TCW 665 Sok Roeu, TCE 12 Chhim Sotheara, TCW 565 Al Rockoff, TCW 384 Leng Chhoeung, TCW 570 Ros Suy, TCW 428 Meas Voeun, TCW 504 Pean Khean, TCW 793 Chhang Youk, TCW 766 Vanthan Dar Peou.

223 The Civil Party Lead Co-Lawyers voluntarily allocated their time for the questioning of TCW-754 Ung Ren to the Office of the Co-Prosecutors.

224 See e.g., Asian International Justice Initiative, *KRT Trial Monitor*, Issue 15, 19-21 March 2012, available online at http://krtmonitor.org/2012/03/21/krt-trial-monitor-issue-no-15/ (last visited 11 March 2015).

225 Studzinsky called the rejection of her submission "arbitrary." As quoted in J. Wallace, "Losing Civil Parties in Cambodia," 143 *International Justice Tribune*, 18 January 2012, at page 2.

226 CPLCLs and CPLs Administrative Internal Regulations, August 2011. Confidential Document.

227 For a comprehensive discussion of the reparations framework, see C. Sperfeldt, "Collective Reparations at the Extraordinary Chambers in the Courts of Cambodia," 12 *International Criminal Law Review*, (2012), 457-489.

227 Extraordinary Chambers in the Courts of Cambodia, Internal Rule 23(1), Revision 6, and further specifications in "Direction on Proceedings Relevant to Reparations and on the Filing of Final Written Submissions," (Case 001/18-07-2007/ECCC/TC), Trial Chamber, 27 August 2009.

228 Twenty-six out of 28 reparations projects initially requested by the Civil Parties were rejected. See Case 001 Judgment, *supra* note 12.

229 The Trial Chamber noted that the Civil Parties did not challenge the determination of indigence at the "trial stage" of the proceedings, thus precluding reparations from being borne against the Accused. Judgment, *Nuon Chea and Khieu Samphan,* (Case 00219-09-2007/ECCC/TC), Trial Chamber, 7 August 2014, at para 1124. However, the Civil Parties did make two requests for investigation into the financial assets of the Accused: one at the investigation stage to the Office of the Co-Investigating Judges and a further request to the Pre-Trial Chamber. Both were rejected.

230 See interview with Nushin Sarkarti in J.D. Ciorciari and A. Heindel, *supra* note 16, at 227.

231 See "Civil Parties' Final Claim for Reparations," (Case 00219-09-2007/ECCC/TC), Trial Chamber, 8 October 2013. All references to the final claim in the Judgment are in French; see Judgment, *Nuon Chea and Khieu Samphan,* (Case 00219-09-2007/ECCC/TC), Trial Chamber, 7 August 2014, at para 1125, fan 3226.

232 Ibid.

233 Extraordinary Chambers in the Courts of Cambodia, Internal Rule 23(1), Revision 8.

234 Case 002/01 Judgment, *supra* note 1, at para 1150.

235 Ibid, at para 1141.

236 Ibid, at 1161.

237 Ibid, at para 1142: the findings on harm appear to reflect an overemphasis on feasibility with limited consideration of the proportionality aspect of the harm suffered.

238 See C. Sperfeldt, "Collective Reparations at the Extraordinary Chambers in the Courts of Cambodia," 12 *International Criminal Law Review*, (2012), 457-489, at 464.

239 "Urgent Request on the Scope of Trial One and the Need for a Reasoned Decision Following the Civil Parties Request for Reconsideration of the Severance Order," (Case 002/19-09-2007-ECCC/TC), Trial Chamber, 17 November 2011.

240 See Case 001 Judgment, *supra* note 12, at para 660.

241 "Urgent Request on the Scope of Trial One and the Need for a Reasoned Decision Following the Civil Parties Request for Reconsideration of the Severance Order," (Case 002/19-09-2007-ECCC/TC), Trial Chamber, 17 November 2011, para 8.

242 This, combined with pending appeals against the Trial Chamber's Severance Orders and the subject matter of Case 002/01, placed the Civil Parties in a constant state of uncertainty. See "Urgent Request on the Scope of Trial One and the Need for a Reasoned Decision Following the Civil Parties Request for Reconsideration of the Severance Order," (Case 002/19-09-2007-ECCC/TC), Trial Chamber, 17 November 2011.

243 Appeal Judgment, *Kaing Guek Eav alias Duch*, (Case 001/18-07-2007/ECCC/SC), Supreme Court Chamber, 3 February 2012, para 659.

244 Case 002/01 Judgment, *supra* note 1, at para 1120.

245 See Decision, *Nuon Chea and Khieu Samphan* (Case 00219-9-2007/ECCC/TC), "Decision on Nuon Chea's Appeal against the Trial Chamber's Decision on Rule 35 Applications for Summary Action," Supreme Court Chamber, 14 September 2012.

246 Judgment, *Prosecutor v Milan Martic,* (IT-95-11 T), ICTY Trial Chamber, 12 June 2007, Table of Contents.

247 Judgment, *Prosecutor v. Sesay, et al.,* (SCSL-04-15-T), SCSL Trial Chamber, 2 March 2009, Table of Contents.

248 Judgment, *Prosecutor v Bagosora, et al.,* (ICTR-98-41-T), ICTR Trial Chamber, 18 December 2008, Table of Contents.

249 Case 002/01 Judgment, *supra* note 1, Table of Contents.

250 Ibid, at para 489.

251 Ibid, at para 520.

252 Ibid, at para 534.

253 Ibid, at para 409.

254 Ibid, at paras 399 and 370. In dealing with the contradictory evidence before it, the Chamber often admits it is unable to make findings on crucial issues. For example, in Paragraph 399 in regard to Khieu Samphan's role in Office 870, the Court considers the various accounts and contradictions and uncertainties, and then concludes that it can make no finding that Khieu Samphan was ever the head of Office 870 or had knowledge of all the communications that passed through that office. This finding undermines putting Khieu Samphan in a key position in what the Judgment has found to be the "nerve center," through which implementing communications went from and to the Standing Committee.

255 Ibid, at para 542.

256 Ibid, at para 655.

257 Ibid, at para 655.

258 Ibid, at para 656.

259 Ibid, at para 634.

260 Ibid, at para 688: The Chamber notes that it will treat superior responsibility as a secondary theory of liability: "Where an accused is found to be both directly responsible and responsible as a superior in relation to the same conduct, the Chamber will convict on the basis of the former and consider an Accused's superior position as an aggravating factor in sentencing."

261 Ibid, at para 941.

262 Ibid.

263 See e.g., C. Damgaard, "The Joint Criminal Enterprise Doctrine: A 'Monster Theory of Liability' or a Legitimate and Satisfactory Tool in the Prosecution of the Perpetrators of Core International Crimes?" in C. Damgaard (ed.), *Individual Criminal Responsibility for Core International Crimes* (Berlin: Springer, 2008), 127-261, at 129.

264 W.A. Schabas, "Mens Rea and the International Criminal Tribunal for the Former Yugoslavia," 37:4 *New England Law Review* (2003), 1015-1036, at 1033-1034.

265 Judgment, *Prosecutor v. Tadić* (IT-94-1-A), ICTY Appeals Chamber, 15 July 1999, paras 185-234.

266 Ibid, at para 190.

267 See Case 002/01 Judgment, *supra* note 1, at paras 690-691.

[268] See Decision, *Ieng Sary, Nuon Chea and Khieu Samphan* (Case 00219-9-2007/ECCC/TC), "Decision on Appeals against the Co-Investigating Judges' Order on Joint Criminal Enterprise (JCE)," Pre/Trial Chamber, 20 May 2010. See also Decision, *Ieng Sary, Ieng Thirith, Nuon Chea and Khieu Samphan* (Case 00219-9-2007/ECCC/TC), "Decision on the Applicability of Joint Criminal Enterprise," Trial Chamber, 12 September 2011.

[269] Case 002/01 Judgment, *supra* note 1, at para 691.

[270] Decision, *Ieng Thirith, Ieng Sary, Khieu Samphan* (Case 00219-9-2007/ECCC/OCIJ), "Decision on the Appeals against the Co-Investigative Judges [sic] Order on Joint Criminal Enterprise (JCE)," Pre-Trial Chamber, 20 May 2010, para 72.

[271] T. Taylor, *Nuremberg and Vietnam: An American Tragedy* (Chicago: Quadrangle Books, 1970).

[272] Case 002/01 Judgment, *supra* note 1, at para 691, providing references to the relevant decisions.

[273] See Judgment, *Prosecutor v. Tadić, supra* note 265, at footnotes 235, 236, 239, 243. The cases cited there had to be obtained by making copies from the original documents at the relevant national archives. The "Tadić Appeal Judgment," at e.g., footnotes 233, 238, 250, 251, 255, also relies heavily on the accounts of trials in the United Nations War Crime Commission (UNWCC) Law Reports of Trials of War Criminals, available at http://www.loc.gov/rr/frd/Military_Law/law-reports-trials-war-criminals.html (visited 7 September 2015), not taking into account that these are not official trial records but rather reports written by individuals sent to observe the trials by the UNWCC. See also the reference to one of the Italian cases relied upon by the Appeals Judgment, indicating its relative inaccessibility: "*See* handwritten text of the (unpublished) judgment, p. 6 (unofficial translation; kindly provided by the Italian Public Record Office, Rome)" at footnote 270. In 1999, when the Berkeley War Crimes Studies Center began working with Italian archives to obtain copies of the post-WWII Italian trial records, we were informed by the Judge Advocate General of the Italian Army that these records were still classified and not yet available to the public.

[274] In 1972-1974, the US National Archives and the British Public Records Office (now English National Archives at Kew Gardens) began the reclassification of WWII records that included the bulk of documents involving war crimes investigations and war crimes trials, available at http://www.archives.gov/research/military/ww2/ (visited 8 September 2015).

[275] Judgment, *Prosecutor v. Kvocka, et al.* (IT-98-30/1-A), ICTY Appeals Chamber, 28 February 2005, at para 117.

[276] See e.g., Judgment, *Prosecutor v. Karamera, et. al.* (ICTR-98-44-A), ICTR Appeals Chamber, 29 September 2014, para 147; Judgment, *Prosecutor v. Elizaphan Ntakirutimana and Gerard Ntakirutimana* (ICTR-96-10-A and ICTR-96-17-A), 13 December 2004, at para 466.

[277] See e.g., *Prosecutor v. Mirolad Krnojelac* (IT-97-25-A), ICTY Appeals Chamber, 17 September 2003, at para 97.

[278] Case 002/01 Judgment, *supra* note 1, at para 722.

[279] Ibid, at para 723.

[280] Ibid, at para 724.

[281] Ibid, at para 725.

[282] Ibid, at para 738.

[283] Ibid, at para 804.

[284] Ibid, at para 805.

[285] See Judgment, *Prosecutor v. Sesay et. al.* (SCSL-04-15-A), SCSL Appeals Chamber, 26 October 2009. For criticism of the Sesay JCE decision, see the "Partially Dissenting and Concurring Opinion of Justice Shireen Avis Fisher" at pages 512-24 of the Appeals Chamber Judgment. See also W. Jordash and P. Van Tuyl, "Failure to Carry the Burden of Proof: How Joint Criminal Enterprise Lost its Way at the Special Court for Sierra Leone," 8:2 *Journal International Criminal Justice* (2010), 591-613.

[286] *United States v. Medina,* CM 427162 (ACMR 1971). Documents from the Medina Court Martial are available at http://law2.umkc.edu/faculty/projects/ftrials/mylai/MYL_MEDT.HTM (visited 8 September 2015).

[287] *U.S. v. Yamashita,* "Records of Trials of Accused Japanese War Criminals Tried at Manila, Phillip Military Commission Convened by the Commanding General of the US Army in the eastern Pacific, 1945-1947" (College Park, Maryland: NARA), Microfilm M1727. For the best recent discussion of the trial of Yamashita Tomoyuki, with full references to relevant materials, see Y. Totani, *Justice in Asia and the Pacific Region, 1945-1952: Allied War Crimes Prosecutions* (1st ed., New York: Cambridge University Press, 2015), 21-40.

[288] See T. Taylor, *Nuremberg and Vietnam: An American Tragedy, supra* note 271, at 182.

[289] "US v. von Leeb et. al.," ("The High Command Case"), in *Trials of War Criminals before the Nuremberg Military Tribunals Vol. X-XI* (Washington DC, US Government Printing Office, 1950).

[290] "US v. List et. al." ("The Hostage Case"), in *Trials of War Criminals before the Nuremberg Military Tribunals Vol. X-XI* (Washington DC, US Government Printing Office, 1950).

[291] *U.S. v. Yamashita*, "Records of Trials of Accused Japanese War Criminals Tried at Manila, Phillip Military Commission Convened by the Commanding General of the US Army in the eastern Pacific, 1945-1947" (College Park, Maryland: NARA), Microfilm M1727. For more information on the Homma Case, see Y. Totani, *Justice in Asia and the Pacific Region, 1945-1952: Allied War Crimes Prosecutions* (1st ed., New York: Cambridge University Press, 2015), 40-46.

[292] "Records of the Trial of Accused War Criminal Soemu Toyoda," (College Park, Maryland: NARA), Microfilm M1729. "Transcripts from the Case of the *United States of America v. Soemu Toyoda and Hiroshi Tamuri*, 1946-1948" (College Park, Maryland: NARA), Microfilm M1661.

[293] See Y. Totani, *Justice in Asia and the Pacific Region 1945-1953: Allied War Crimes Prosecutions* (New York, Cambridge University Press 2015), 77-178.

[294] Judgment, *Prosecutor v Delalic, et al.* ("Čelebići Case") (IT-96-21-A), Appeals Chamber, 20 February 2001, pages 54-104.

[295] Ibid, pages 121-147.

[296] Case 002/01 Judgment, *supra* note 1, at para 719.

[297] Ibid, at para 207.

[298] The confusion among expert witnesses appears further from the testimony of Heder in Case 002/01 Judgment, *supra* note 1, at para 212; see also para 199, Administrative Structures, which begins with the statement that, "The precise operational structure of the CPK was shrouded in secrecy."

[299] See e.g., Case 002/01 Judgment, *supra* note 1, at paras 221-222.

[300] Ibid, at para 228.

[301] Ibid, at para 142.

[302] Ibid, at para 135.

[303] Ibid, at para 138. See also the Separate Opinion of Judge Orie on the key distinction of a finding of "likelihood" on the one hand, and the proof required to meet the reasonable doubt standard on the other in Judgment, *Prosecutor v Stanisic et al.* (IT-03-69-T), ICTY Trial Chamber, 30 May 2013, at pages 870-871.

[304] Case 002/01 Judgment, *supra* note 1, at para 143.

[305] Ibid, at footnote 425.

[306] Ibid.

[307] Ibid, at para 228.

[308] Ibid, at para 378: "The Chamber is unable to say whether KHIEU Samphan retained the title of Commander-in-Chief when the CPNLAF was reformed into the RAK in July 1975. In any event, the Chamber is satisfied that KHIEU Samphan never had direct military responsibilities. He did, however, attend meetings with other CPK/DK senior leaders and military commanders or Zone or Sector-level officials at which military matters were discussed." What inferences can be made in regard to military actions from the fact that he was present at some such meetings when we do not know in what capacity or what his role was beyond, for example, observer for informational purposes?

[309] Ibid, at para 370, which discusses a Khmer Rouge press release stating that Khieu Samphan had presided at a meeting where it was decided that the "7 traitors" had to be killed. The court concludes, however, that the evidence is inconclusive as to whether such a meeting ever took place.

[310] Ibid, at para 152.

[311] Compare the Chamber's methodology, for example, with the extended discussion of such issues in the ICTY *Stanisic* and *Gotovina* Cases. In *Prosecutor v Stanisic et al.*, ICTY IT-03-69-T, Trial Chamber, 30 May 2013, the Trial Chamber acquitted the Accused. After findings that crimes alleged in the Indictment had indeed been committed, the Trial Chamber carefully reviewed the testimony of each witness bearing upon the connection of the Accused to those crimes. This review, encompassing almost 400 pages (pp. 460-820), represents the kind of meticulous analysis and weighing of the evidence that is almost entirely absent in the Judgment of Case 002/1. In regard to the participation of Stanisic in a JCE I and his alleged liability under JCE III, the Stanisic Judgment found that even if the crimes committed were foreseeable, the crucial issue was whether the Accused shared the criminal intent, as required by the JCE I, to commit those crimes. The Chamber found that the evidence was ambiguous on this issue and admitted of

multiple inferences. As Judge Orie explained in his Separate Opinion, although one permissible inference was that Stanisic shared the intent, "That would not be the only reasonable inference to be drawn from the evidence presented." (p. 870) Judge Orie continued to explain in regard to the burden of proof that, "My task is not to assess what was *likely* the intent of the Accused but whether the evidence allows me to establish *beyond a reasonable doubt* what they intended." (p. 871) Compare also the detailed analysis and weighing of all the relevant evidence for each crime site in *Prosecutor v Gotovina, et al.*, ICTY IT 06-90-T, 15 April 2011, pages 105-799.

[312] Case 002/01 Judgment, *supra* note 1, at para 385.

[313] Ibid, at para 385.

[314] Ibid, at para 386.

[315] Ibid, at para 387.

[316] Ibid, at para 739.

[317] Ibid, at para 740.

[318] Ibid, at para 746.

[319] Ibid, at para 747.

[320] Ibid.

[321] Ibid, at para 757.

[322] Ibid, at para 768: "Meanwhile, the Standing Committee continued meeting concerning implementation of the Party's political line and administration of the country. Minutes of meetings held between August 1975 and June 1976, and indicating attendance of various party leaders, were put before the Chamber. The Standing Committee and at times other senior leaders who were not members of the committee including KHIEU Samphan, IENG Thirith and various Zone and Autonomous Sector secretaries, considered and decided upon matters relating to propaganda and foreign affairs; commerce and trade; national defence; and economic matters …" We see here the continuing lack of precision as to Khieu Samphan's attendance at specific meetings, as well as his role and the roles of any individuals. The formulation is again extremely vague: The Standing Committee "and at times" others "including Khieu Sampan" considered and decided … Who decided what and how did Khieu Samphan participate or not? What did he say that connects him to the JCE and manifests his intent that the crimes charged be carried out as the means by which the socialist revolution was implemented?

[323] Ibid, at para 748.

[324] See *supra* Part II.B.

[325] Case 002/01 Judgment, *supra* note 1, at para 868-869, 902.

[326] Ibid, at paras 746-753.

[327] Ibid, at para 748.

[328] Ibid, at para 749. Note that the neither the reasonable doubt standard nor what other inferences might reasonably be drawn from the evidence is ever mentioned in the discussion of this document and related meetings.

[329] Ibid, at para 749.

[330] Ibid, at para 750.

[331] Ibid, at para 751.

[332] Ibid, at para 753.

[333] Ibid, at para 787. The Chamber finds that Nuon Chea and Pol Pot viewed the cities as harboring the enemy ruling classes. Linking Khieu Samphan to such sentiments that state that, "In speeches, KHIEU Samphan endorsed this suspicion and distrust …" The cited speech states that they must oppose colonialism and imperialism, which is found in the ruling classes in Phnom Penh, and that this culture will "eat away" at their sovereignty if they do not oppose it. This is standard socialist cant and does not show an endorsement of anything other than the same socialist revolution that has been stated as the common purpose over and over again in the Judgment. Endorsing suspicion and distrust of the imperialist/colonialist classes is hardly evidence of shared intent to commit the crimes charged.

[334] Ibid, at para 788.

[335] Ibid, at para 798.

[336] See *infra* Part III.B.3 discussing findings on Nuon Chea and Khieu Samphan's respective specific liability.

[337] Case 002/01 Judgment, *supra* note 1, at paras 808-810.

[338] Ibid, at para 810.

[339] Ibid, at para 813.

[340] Ibid.

[341] Decision, *Ieng Sary, Ieng Thirith, Khieu Samphan* (Case 00219-9-2007/ECCC/OCIJ [PTC38]), "Decision on the Appeals Against the Co-Investigative Judges Order on Joint Criminal Enterprise (JCE)," Pre-Trial Chamber, 20 May 2010.

[342] Case 002/01 Judgment, *supra* note 1, at paras 814-818.

[343] Ibid, at para 815.

[344] Ibid, at para 815, citing: Trial Chamber Transcript, 13 December 2011 (KHIEU Samphan), page 95. ("The people and Revolutionary Army were alerted to the true nature of the aggressive and annexationist, cruel and treacherous American imperialists and their lackeys who were the enemies of the people. The people were constantly on revolutionary alert.")

[345] Ibid, at para 816.

[346] Ibid, at para 816: "During a meeting in June 1974, at which the Central Committee planned the final offensive to liberate the country, NUON Chea, POL Pot, KHIEU Samphan, Zone, Sector and military leaders discussed the Party's experience at Oudong, where Khmer Republic officials were executed en masse. Having considered this prior 'success,' the Party leadership decided on its strategy for the final offensive. This plan was affirmed during meetings in early April 1975."

[347] Ibid at para 146, regarding the credibility of witness Phy Phuon.

[348] Ibid, at paras 830-834, regarding a "pattern" in these killings. Khieu Samphan only appears once, as having made a statement on 21 April 1975 "that the army had succeeded in 'relentlessly attacking and draining the enemy' who had died in agony." Given that he says it was the army that had attacked the enemy, and the enemy is not specified and the country viewed itself as at war, this hardly connects him either to the policy or to the "pattern" of killing Khmer Republic leaders. The conclusion of this section is that three expert witnesses confirmed that a policy to eliminate Khmer Republic officials was implemented "nationwide." There is no indication that these witnesses linked Khieu Samphan to that policy and this final concluding sentence names no individuals. The preceding paragraphs rely merely on general attribution to "the Party."

[349] Ibid, at para 835.

[350] See e.g., Judgment, *Prosecutor v Radoslav Krstic*, (Case IT-98-33A), ICTY Appeals Chamber, 19 April 2004, 26-29.

[351] Case 002/01 Judgment, *supra* note 1, at para 839.

[352] Ibid, at para 846.

[353] Ibid, at para 846.

[354] Ibid, at para 849.

[355] Ibid, at para 869.

[356] Ibid, at para 875-876.

[357] Ibid, at para 876.

[358] See *supra* Part III.B.3.a.

[359] Case 002/01 Judgment, *supra* note 1, at para 876.

[360] Ibid, at paras 917, and 921-922: The Chamber returns to the issue of Nuon Chea's liability for the killings at Tuol Po Chrey. Although this section is devoted to "planning" as a mode of liability, the analysis is again formulated in the language of JCE III, though it does not refer to that doctrine. The key element on which the Chamber's conclusion of liability for planning is grounded is that it was foreseeable to Nuon Chea that crimes would be committed because of the general policies to which he allegedly contributed. In Paragraph 919, the Chamber focuses on Khmer Rouge general policies grounded in "secrecy" and "indoctrination." They state that senior leaders such as Nuon Chea and Khieu Samphan were aware of the "substantial likelihood" that crimes would result from these policies. On this basis they conclude that, "as a general matter, the plans necessarily involved and contemplated that crimes would be committed on a large scale, including at Tuol Po Chrey." The final paragraphs (921-922) of this section clarify what is apparently meant by the vague phrase "as a general matter." Here the Chamber specifies that "in planning the final offensive to liberate the country Nuon Chea intended or was aware of a substantial likelihood of the commission of

these crimes." On this basis the Chamber maintains that liability for murder and extermination as crimes against humanity may be established on the basis of recklessness (conscious disregard of a risk) as the *mens rea* in regard to general policies which may result in the commission of such crimes.

[361] Judgment, *Prosecutor v Kunarac et al.,* (IT-96-23-T and 96-23/1-T), ICTY Trial Chamber, 22 February 2001, pages 216-217, holding that the Prosecution must prove effective control at the time that the direct perpetrators committed the underlying offense.

[362] See *infra* Part III.B.3 for further discussion.

[363] Case 002/01 Judgment, *supra* note 1, at para 892.

[364] Ibid, at para 892.

[365] See *supra* note 249 for further discussion of troubling legal foundations of Superior Responsibility.

[366] Case 002/01 Judgment, *supra* note 1, at para 893.

[367] Ibid, at para 894.

[368] Ibid, at para 894.

[369] Ibid, at para 913: where the Chamber again concludes that Nuon Chea exercised effective control over "*all* Khmer Rouge cadres" (emphasis added) because of the "strict reporting line through which the lower echelons briefed senior leaders on key matters and requested guidance." Here again, rather than focusing on the specific authority of Nuon Chea, the Chamber lumps him together with "the senior leaders" and suggests that each one of them was a superior of all the Khmer Rouge units and formations because of the "strict reporting line." Apart from the fact that it does not individuate the specific role and authority of Nuon Chea, its own narrative of the Khmer Rouge and the dissension and repression of various cadres has indicated that there never was such a monolithic structure of *de facto* authority over all Khmer Rouge cadres at all times and in regard to all crimes, which is what is implied here and in the sweeping conclusion of Paragraph 917.

[370] Case 002/01 Judgment, *supra* note 1, at para 941.

[371] Ibid, at para 960.

[372] Ibid at Section 16.1.1.

[373] Ibid, at para 952.

[374] Ibid, at para 604.

[375] Ibid, at para 606.

[376] Ibid, beginning at para 964.

[377] Ibid, at para 972.

[378] Ibid, at para 228.

[379] Ibid, at para 972.

[380] Ibid, at para 152.

[381] ibid, at paras 993-995.

[382] Ibid, at para 995.

Acknowledgments

This report was made possible by the formidable work of the Asian International Justice Initiative's (AIJI) Khmer Rouge Tribunal (KRT) Monitoring Group, with vital research assistance (including trial data compilation and preliminary analysis) from many former trial monitors and student interns who worked with AIJI at various points since Case 002/01 first began. The report is based, in part, on the observations and insights of these individuals and other members of the monitoring team who collectively covered the courtroom proceedings the entire duration of the trial. The co-authors wish to thank: Yumna Arif, Mary Kristerie A. Baleva, Stewart Beck, Borany Bon, Gemma Chew, Chhaya Chhin, Phalla Chhoeun, Pheakdey Chum, Adair Fincher, Nora Fuchs, Jacob Garner, Samuel Gilg, Francisca Gilmore, Thilo Gottschalk, Andrew Grant, Piseth Huy, Judith Kaiser, Sadaf Kashfi, Kounila Keo, Faith Suzzette Delos Reyes Kong, Anne Lang, Samantha Lee, Gabrielle Lindsay, Daniel Mattes, Jessica Mawrence, Havi Mirell, Aviva Nababan, Ramu Nachiappan, Pavithra Prakash Nair, Vidjia Phun, Princess B. Principe, John Reiss, Leonie Rodger, Tobias Roemer, Noyel Ry, Joy Scott, Sovanna Sek, Elodie Somerville, Kosal Sor, Sonan Sorn, Sarun Sous, Kimsan Soy, Juan Pablo Stein, Lucy Sullivan, Chhayrath Tan, Austin Tang, Lina Tay, Stephanie Teh, Chayanich Thamparipattra, Flavia Widmer, Elin Wong, and Alvin Yap, as well as Christoph Sperfeldt who provided helpful comment on early drafts of the report.

At the East-West Center, thanks to the Research Program's director, Nancy Lewis, staff, and publications team—Elisa Johnston, Lillian Shimoda, and Carol Wong—for patient support and guidance over the last year.

Last but certainly not least, the co-authors wish to extend a very special thanks to Stephanie Fung, a former AIJI trial monitor who returned to work with us this year, providing valuable research assistance and comments throughout the report drafting process, as well as copy editing right up to the end.

About the Authors

David Cohen is a leading expert in the fields of human rights, international law, and transitional justice. He taught at University of California Berkeley from 1979 to 2012 as the Ancker Distinguished Professor for the Humanities, and served as the founding director of the Berkeley War Crimes Studies Center (WCSC), which moved to Stanford University at the end of 2013 and became the WSD HANDA Center for Human Rights and International Justice. Cohen is a professor of Law at the William S. Richardson School of Law, University of Hawai`i; a senior fellow at the East-West Center; a professor in the Graduate School at UC Berkeley; and a visiting professor at Stanford. His involvement in research in war crimes tribunals began in the mid-1990s with a project to collect the records of the national war crimes programs conducted in approximately 20 countries in Europe and Asia after WWII. Since 2001, Cohen's work has largely focused on contemporary tribunals and transitional justice initiatives. Cohen has led justice-sector reform initiatives and tribunal- monitoring programs in Indonesia, East Timor, Sierra Leone, Bangladesh, Rwanda, and Cambodia. Cohen received his JD at UCLA's School of Law, and his PhD in classics and ancient history from Cambridge University.

Melanie Hyde is an Australian human rights lawyer, with a master's degree in Law from the University of Melbourne and a bachelor's degree in Arts and Law from the University of Queensland. Currently based in Phnom Penh, Hyde serves as the head of Cambodian Programs for the WSD HANDA Center and the East-West Center's Asian International Justice Initiative (AIJI). She is responsible for coordinating a range of programs in Cambodia, including the AIJI Khmer Rouge Tribunal Monitoring Program at the Extraordinary Chambers in the Courts of Cambodia, the Voices for Reconciliation Program, the *Facing Justice* television series, and various legal education initiatives related to rule of law and transitional justice. She has developed university curriculum and taught courses on human rights and criminal justice in several Cambodian universities. Prior to joining AIJI, Hyde worked on gender justice and equality initiatives in Australia, Afghanistan, Cameroon, Cambodia, and Libya.

Penelope Van Tuyl is an American human rights lawyer. She received her JD from the University of California, Berkeley School of Law, and is admitted to practice in the state of California. She has worked closely with David Cohen for nearly a decade on human rights and rule of law projects around the world. As associate director for the WSD HANDA Center for Human Rights and International Justice (and, previously, the War Crimes Studies Center), Van Tuyl has overseen many of the Center's key justice initiatives, including trial monitoring programs and the development of innovative digital platforms for archival war crimes trial records. Van Tuyl has authored and edited numerous reports and articles on international criminal law and procedure. At UC Berkeley, she has also developed and taught undergraduate courses in human rights and international law, which she brought to Stanford University when WCSC became the Handa Center. Her research interests touch on substantive, procedural, and administrative aspects of international criminal law practice; in particular, she focuses on Joint Criminal Enterprise liability, standards of pleading in international courts, and the institutional accountability mechanisms that are meant to support the effective and efficient administration of justice.

About the Research Supporters and Publishers

The **East-West Center** promotes better relations and understanding among the people and nations of the United States, Asia, and the Pacific through cooperative study, research, and dialogue. Established by the US Congress in 1960, the Center serves as a resource for information and analysis on critical issues of common concern, bringing people together to exchange views, build expertise, and develop policy options. The Center's 21-acre Honolulu campus, adjacent to the University of Hawai'i at Mānoa, is located midway between Asia and the US mainland and features research, residential, and international conference facilities. The Center's Washington, DC, office focuses on preparing the United States for an era of growing Asia Pacific prominence.

EastWestCenter.org

The **WSD HANDA Center for Human Rights and International Justice** is dedicated to promoting the rule of law, accountability, and human rights around the world, in post-conflict settings, developing countries, and in societies grappling with difficult legacies from a historical period of violent conflict. Through research and international programs, the Handa Center supports and helps improve the work of domestic courts, international tribunals, and human rights commissions around the world. Relying on a small core group of lawyers, scholars, student interns, and volunteers, the Center concentrates its resources where it can make a real difference helping people make sense of the past, come to terms with periods of violent social upheaval, and build institutions that will promote justice and accountability. The Center is further committed to increasing awareness and raising the level of discourse around new developments in the fields of human rights and international law. To this end, the Handa Center has dedicated itself to becoming a major public resource center for the study of war crimes and human rights trials, where students, scholars, and legal practitioners can take advantage of new technologies to access unique archival resources from World War II through contemporary international criminal trials.

HandaCenter.Stanford.edu

The **Asian International Justice Initiative** (AIJI) focuses on projects and partnerships related to international justice, judicial reform, the rule of law, and human rights in ASEAN and other Asia-Pacific countries. AIJI is a nearly decade-old collaboration between the East-West Center (EWC) and the WSD HANDA Center for Human Rights and International Justice at Stanford University (previously known as the Berkeley War Crimes Studies Center). AIJI combines the Asia-Pacific regional expertise of the EWC and the transitional justice research and human rights training capabilities of the Handa Center. AIJI was formed in recognition of the joint aim of the parties to foster initiatives in the Asia Pacific (or for Asia-Pacific partners) that promote standards of excellence in international justice and human rights as practiced throughout the region. Under the AIJI umbrella, the Handa Center and the EWC work in close partnership with regional and country-specific institutions to implement programs that generally promote human rights education, understanding and awareness of internationally recognized fair trial standards, and requirements for the accountability and the rule of law, especially in international criminal trials and human rights proceedings in national courts.

EastWestCenter.org/AIJI
HandaCenter.Stanford.edu

www.ingramcontent.com/pod-product-compliance
Lightning Source LLC
Chambersburg PA
CBHW081409270326
41931CB00016B/3427